Effective Case Analysis

Techniques for Success in Case-based Learning and Examinations

Alan J. Richardson | Odette School of Business
University of Windsor

Captus Press

Effective Case Analysis: Techniques for Success in Case-based
Learning and Examinations

Captus Press Inc.
Mail: Units 14 & 15, 1600 Steeles Avenue West
       Concord, Ontario
       L4K 4M2
Tel: (416) 736–5537
Fax: (416) 736–5793
Email: info@captus.com
Internet: www.captus.com

Library and Archives Canada Cataloguing in Publication

Richardson, Alan J. (Alan John), 1955–, author
   Effective case analysis : techniques for success in
case-based learning and examinations / Alan J. Richardson.

Includes bibliographical references and index.
ISBN 978-1-55322-280-4

1. Case-based reasoning. 2. Research — Methodology.
I. Title.

Q338.8.R53 2013   153.4'3   C2013-902561-8-0

Canada   We acknowledge the financial support of
the Government of Canada through the
Canada Book Fund for our publishing activities.

0 9 8 7 6 5 4 3 2 1
Printed in Canada

Contents

Contents

List of Figures and Tables

List of Figures

List of Tables

Preface and Acknowledgements

This brief text is based on my experience writing cases, teaching with cases in undergraduate and graduate programs, and developing material to teach case analysis to MBA students. The goal of this book is to integrate case learning with the techniques for decision-making that have become common across a range of disciplines. The book is based on the premise that decision-makers/case analysts dealing with complex and ambiguous circumstances prefer to make rational decisions but are hampered by unconscious cognitive biases and procedural blinders that restrict their identification of issues and alternatives, and may bias the evaluation of those alternatives. This book seeks to integrate systematic case analysis with techniques that reduce and make visible potential biases in decision-making. The emphasis in this book is on "appropriate technologies"[1] for decision-making, i.e., technologies that acknowledge the data limitations and complexity of real decisions and provide tools that are simple to implement but powerful in their ability to overcome bias. The book is richly illustrated to provide memorable images and examples to reinforce learning.

I am grateful to the students in my management control systems course at Queen's University and York University, to participants in the case analysis workshops presented as part of the Schulich MBA "Fast Start" program and the University of Windsor MBA Orientation, and to

---

[1] The concept of "appropriate technology" refers to the simplest level of technology that can serve an intended purpose. This concept was developed in the context of technology transfer to the developing world where solutions to problems in developed economies proved too expensive and complex for problems in less developed countries. The use of the term here is a reaction to a range of texts on decision-making that are based on complex statistical models and require very precise data to be operationalized. The cases that most analysts are faced with do not have the data or the simple structures that these models require so the intent is to present techniques that will work with the level of data faced by most case analysts. Obviously, where data allows, more sophisticated means of doing the analysis should be used as an adjunct to the process described in this text.

the contributors to my edited case books in financial and managerial accounting (published by Nelson Publishing) who have helped to refine my views of case-based learning. My entrée into writing teaching materials was provided by the late Charles Horngren and Rod Banister (initially with Prentice Hall, then Nelson Thomson); I thank them for the opportunity. I would also like to acknowledge the comments of Eksa Kilfoyle (University of Windsor), Brian Jones (Quinnipiac University), Elizabeth Farrell (York University) and the reviewers of earlier versions of this text.

This book is intended primarily for students in accounting and business programs. The techniques described, however, apply to any case based learning environment, and would also be useful to those in practice who routinely make decisions in complex and ambiguous contexts.

1 Introduction

Case-based learning — also referred to as problem-based learning — and case-based examination processes have always been common in professional disciplines such as medicine, law and business. In business, in particular, cases are an important tool for exposing students to the complexities of management decision-making and for developing the critical thinking skills that managers exercise every day. In spite of the centrality of case-based learning and examination processes in business education, there is little formal guidance for case analysis, and that which is available tends to provide a high level framework for structuring the analysis without providing the tools to do the work. But since the introduction of cases into the curriculum of professional schools, our understanding of the psychology of decision-making and decision-making techniques has developed considerably, and it is appropriate that we integrate the decision aides and techniques that have been developed in various fields into the learning process itself.

This short book is intended to fill that gap; to identify and illustrate a set of techniques that can significantly improve each stage in the case analysis process. These techniques play two roles. First, in many instances the techniques provide a systematic way of implementing the basic logic of case analysis. The techniques are intended to act as checklists and guidelines to ensure that all aspects of case analysis are considered and done well. Second, the techniques in this book are also designed to help overcome many of the group and individual biases in decision-making that have been identified by researchers.

Research in many fields has confirmed that decision-makers are "intendedly rational" but subject to various cognitive and procedural biases that limit their ability to make rational decisions in all circumstances. Appendix A summarizes some of these biases. As our knowledge of these biases grows, we have developed techniques to minimize their impact or

---

This chapter is based on Chapter 1, pp. 1–6 from Richardson, A.J. *Cases in Financial Accounting*, *1e* © 2007 Nelson Education Ltd. Reproduced by permission <www.cengage.com/permissions>.

raise their visibility to allow us to correct these biases. Many of the techniques in this book serve the important role of helping case analysts make better decisions by overcoming their innate cognitive limitations.

In this introductory Chapter, I will review the variety of types of cases and identify the type of case to which the techniques in this book apply. I will then lay out the pedagogic and professional rationales for the use of case-based learning and examinations and provide a road map for the remainder of the book. This chapter reinforces the importance of case-based learning in your future career and makes clear what you should be getting out of this form of educational experience. Our starting point, however, is with a basic question: what is a case?[1]

What is a Case?

The term "case" is used to refer to many things in an academic context, so it is important at the outset to clarify the type of case to which this book applies. I will distinguish between four types of "cases" based on the objective of each type.

1. Research Cases: Academic researchers often use "case studies" as a method to gain understanding of complex phenomena. Sometimes researchers will use multiple case studies with each case selected to help explore a particular dimension of a theory or phenomenon. These cases are written to reflect the theoretical or empirical insights that the researcher has gained from the case study.

2. Illustrative Cases: Textbook writers are increasingly concerned to link their material to real-world examples and provide brief descriptions of specific cases to illustrate a concept or phenomenon. For example, a discussion of brand value would probably include reference to Coca-Cola, Harley Davidson or Apple as specific cases (examples) of successful brand management. These cases provide a concrete example of some phenomenon of interest, with the objective of creating a more lasting impression than could be achieved with a more abstract form of presentation. Textbook writers may also illustrate generic techniques or processes with specific examples from a company. For example, if a textbook was trying to illustrate effective supply-chain management, the author may provide details of how Wal-Mart handles their suppliers or they may use Shell Oil as an example of state-of-the-art sustainability reporting.

3. Exercise Cases: In many recent textbooks, cases were added to the end-of-chapter material that can be used as assignments or practice with particular techniques. These are really disguised numeric problems that provide a description of the context but allow for a single right answer.

---

[1] This typology is modified from Gill, T. Grandon (2012). "Writing Case Studies Checklist", University of South Florida.

4. Discussion Cases: The type of case to which this book applies is intended as a vehicle for discussion and analysis. A good discussion case, like real world problems, is rich in detail and allows for many possible solutions. It should allow for different perspectives on the events described and provide a context for the use of critical thinking skills. These cases are usually (but not always) based on real situations faced by managers that required action in the face of uncertainty and ambiguity.

The case method of instruction was first used at Harvard Law School in 1870 and brought into the Harvard Business School in 1920.[2] Cases were used as examples from which general principles of professional practice could be inferred. In the law school, cases referred to the decisions of judges on specific cases and the intent was for law students to understand how judges used the law. In the business school the type of case changed to provide rich descriptions of actual business issues that could form the basis for student analysis and recommendation. The business case is the equivalent of the laboratory in natural sciences.[3] The instructor in a traditional case classroom uses the Socratic method of teaching, i.e., they ask questions to help students explore the case and come to their own conclusions. The use of cases has subsequently spread across many professional schools and the approach to case analysis has developed to reflect both theoretical and technical advances in decision-making.

Discussion cases may range from a few pages in length to documents of over 50 pages. The key characteristic is that discussion cases provide an opportunity for you to practice your critical thinking skills in a context that allows for alternative solutions.

The Case for Cases

One of the common reactions of students to the use of cases in the classroom is that it is an inefficient way to learn. Students just want the instructor to get to the point and tell them the "lesson" from the case. Certainly if the point of a lecture is to convey factual information, then there are better ways to present the material than engaging in a many-faceted discussion of specific cases. But cases are used to develop and practice the skills managers and professionals need in their daily practice and to teach an approach to complex and ambiguous problems that goes beyond factual knowledge. The strength of case-based learning and examination processes has been recognized in both pedagogic and professional settings.

---

[2] Garvin, D.A. (2003). "Making the case", *Harvard Magazine* V106 N1: 56–58.

[3] See Jones, D.G.B. and Monieson, D.D. (1988). "The Origin and Early Development of the Case Method in Marketing Pedagogy", *Developments in Marketing Science* (Bahn, K. Ed.) V XI.

The Pedagogic Case for Cases

One of the important roles of a classroom instructor (a role that students may not see or appreciate) is to choose the way in which the course subject matter is explored by students. In some situations, students may be expected to work through material on their own, in other situations group work will be encouraged; in some classes the instructor will present material, hoping to provide structure and clarity to difficult material, in other classes the instructor will use cases and engage students in a conversation about the material. Each choice reflects the specific pedagogic objectives of the instructor in interaction with the nature of the material and the capabilities of the students. The decision to use cases reflects the instructor's desire to help students develop critical thinking skills in the context of ambiguous and complex material. The skills that are developed in case analysis can best be understood in the context of Bloom's hierarchy of learning objectives.[4]

Bloom suggests that learning develops through six levels: knowledge, comprehension, application, analysis, synthesis and evaluation. In addition, learning also involves three domains: cognitive, affective and psychomotor. In other words, to fully learn something you must understand it (the cognitive domain — represented by Bloom's taxonomy), value it (the affective domain) and be able to use it (the psychomotor domain). In Bloom's taxonomy "knowledge" refers to the basic vocabulary of the field and the referents of key terms and categories used to organize the field. "Comprehension" refers to an understanding of the meaning of knowledge and the logic that underlies differences between categories. "Application" refers to an ability to use knowledge in well-structured situations (e.g., knowing how to plug numbers into a formulae to get a solution to a problem) and to know when specific bodies of knowledge should be used. "Analyze" refers to the ability to translate knowledge into new settings and to infer relationships within complex data sets. "Synthesis" refers to the ability to combine knowledge from different fields and to be able to construct alternatives for action based on combinations of different concepts or experiences. "Evaluation" refers to the ability to justify and defend actions and the ability to assess the quality of action compared with social and personal values. In recent applications of the framework, a "create" category has been added, referring to the ability to generate new knowledge.

Bloom's taxonomy is sometimes displayed as a wheel, or "rose", as in Figure 1, to capture the idea that learning involves constant cycling among levels. In other words, throughout your life you will constantly be exposed to new knowledge so that mastering one subject (i.e., getting to stage 6 with respect to this subject) provides the starting point for learning something new. Each time you encounter a new subject you will have to begin at stage 1, and learn a new vocabulary, and then move through the cycle again until you master this new subject. With luck, you will never stop

[4] Bloom, B.S., Engelhart, M.D., Furst, E.J., Hill, W.H., & Krathwohl, D.R. (1956). *Taxonomy of educational objectives: the classification of educational goals; Handbook I: Cognitive Domain*. New York, Longmans, Green.

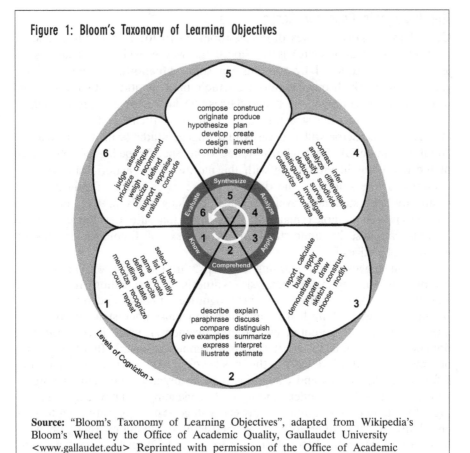

Figure 1: Bloom's Taxonomy of Learning Objectives

Source: "Bloom's Taxonomy of Learning Objectives", adapted from Wikipedia's Bloom's Wheel by the Office of Academic Quality, Gaullaudet University <www.gallaudet.edu> Reprinted with permission of the Office of Academic Quality, Gallaudet University.

learning! In this Figure, the inner ring lists the six learning objectives that form Bloom's hierarchy, while the outer ring provides words that indicate the type of thinking/questions that would reflect each level of learning.

Each level of learning is best supported by different forms of educational experiences. For example, "knowledge" can most efficiently be transferred by readings or lectures and is tested by objective questions of rote memory (e.g., "What are the six levels of Bloom's Hierarchy" would be a question testing "knowledge"); comprehension is developed by using knowledge to create displays or presentations and is tested by asking students to explain concepts or to paraphrase definitions (e.g., "Explain why comprehension is regarded as a higher level of learning than knowledge in Bloom's hierarchy" would be a question testing comprehension); application requires structured problem-solving and is tested by having students use rules to generate solutions with well-structured inputs (e.g., "Identify what level of Bloom's hierarchy the question, 'What are the six levels of Bloom's hierarchy' is intended to test" would be a test of application skills). These three levels are regarded as the basic or lower levels of learning. Most higher education, including professional education, seeks to build learning objectives around the higher levels of Bloom's hierarchy.

Cases are often used when the instructor wishes students to engage with a subject at the higher levels of this taxonomy, i.e., to analyze, synthesize and evaluate material. Cases do this by presenting a complex reality in which students are usually asked to take on the role of a decision-maker and recommend a course of action. (Another format is to ask students to evaluate a decision taken by a decision-maker in the case.) Students must analyze the situation (including the use of technical skills learned previously), synthesize multiple sources of information, and evaluate possible courses of action leading to a recommendation. If the case has been well chosen, there should be no "right" answer; many different recommendations could be offered and many courses of action could have worked in the situation. **The key learning experience is not the answer emerging from your analysis of the case; it is the process by which you get to an answer.** It is this process that is the focus of this book.

Case analysis is thus an important teaching device that provides instructors and students an opportunity to engage with higher level learning objectives in a context that mirrors the future career path of students.

The Professional Case for Cases

The use of cases in the classroom provides a realistic preview of the types of decisions made by managers and professionals in their careers. Cases are used in medical, legal, and business education (among other fields) for precisely this reason. Cases provide you with an opportunity to practice making decisions that would affect the health and welfare of companies and individuals without the risk and stress actually involved in those decisions. For example, cases can be presented that allow you to make multi-million dollar investments, to choose the strategic direction of a company, or to hire or fire key personnel. Most professional schools will ultimately provide you with opportunities to work in the field under supervision (e.g., practicums, placements, internships, field studies, etc.); but short of this type of experience, cases (and simulations to a certain extent) come as close to the reality of the field as possible in the classroom.

Given this potential with cases, it should not be surprising that many professional bodies use case-based examinations (or "simulations", as they are often referred to) to test a candidate's readiness to practice in a field. These examinations will present candidates with realistic examples of situations experienced by entry level practitioners and provide an opportunity for the candidate to demonstrate their mastery of the technical, critical thinking and communications skills that are expected of someone entering the field. This type of examination is used in a wide range of fields including accounting and auditing, project management, financial analysis, financial planning and information systems design (e.g., Microsoft Certified Systems Engineer examinations), among others.

It is also becoming common for consulting firms and investment banking firms to use cases or scenarios to test a candidate's abilities. Since this is usually done in face-to-face interviews the format is a little different from professional examinations. In this setting, the skills of case analysis are tested by asking you to interact with the interviewer as you think through a question that is rich in connotation. The type of question asked in case-based interviews might seem bizarre if you don't expect it.[5] For example, firms have asked questions like, "How many bicycles are there in China", "How many piano tuners are there in Toronto", and other equally unlikely questions.[6] One scenario I have used in case analysis workshops is to ask students to consider a maker of incandescent light bulbs thinking of entering the Australian market and to estimate the size of that market.

If you can Google the answer, you are asking the wrong question.

Two things should be immediately obvious about such questions: first, the interviewer really doesn't care about the answer, and, second, if they did then you might ask to spend a few minutes with Google before answering. What the interviewer is looking for is your ability not to panic when faced with a stressful situation and the ability to approach a problem logically combining general knowledge and reasonable assumptions to reach a conclusion. They are not looking for factual knowledge.

For example, students considering the size of the Australian market for incandescent light bulbs might start with the idea that light bulbs are bought with new fixtures and to replace old bulbs that have burnt out so they would need to estimate the current stock of light bulbs in service and the average life of light bulbs as well as the growth in the market for light fixtures. They might speculate that incandescent bulbs are primarily used in residences rather than in commercial and institutional contexts (or ask the interviewer if this is the target market — clarifying the question is fair game in this type of interview settings, and is also taken as a reflection of your care for satisfying the client) and so estimate the size of the market by estimating the population of Australia, the average family size, the average number of rooms per house, and the average number of light bulbs per room. Estimates of the growth in the population of Australia could be combined with these numbers to estimate the demand from new fixtures (assuming that new fixtures are used when new housing is built and that new housing requires a growth in the population rather than changes in other assumptions, such as average family size etc.). The ability to identify these types of factors, to make reasonable assumptions to fill in missing information, and to develop a logical/reasonable estimate of the market, shows that the interviewee possesses a logic and rigour that seems to relate to career success.

[5] For further examples see: <http://casequestions.com/caseprep.cfm>.

[6] For other examples see: Boston Consulting Group <http://www.bcg.com>; Bain and Company <http://www.joinbain.com>; and McKinsey <http://www.mckinsey.com/>.

One of the reasons that I like the example of estimating the Australian market for incandescent light bulbs is that in this case there is a correct answer: zero. In 2007 Australia passed a law banning the sale of incandescent light bulbs after 2010 in an effort to reduce greenhouse gases. As long as this is not part of the general knowledge of students, then the exercise is valid and reinforces the idea that the answer was not important — the process of trying to answer the question was the real test. This is the same with case analysis: it is not the recommendation that is important; it is the process by which you get to that recommendation. It is the journey that is important; not the destination. Keep this in mind as you go through this book and during interviews and professional examinations that use cases; focus on the process and the outcome will take care of itself.

Case analysis is thus a skill that managers and professionals use every day to serve clients and reason through major decisions. Case examinations and case-based interviews are used by many employers and professional associations to test whether a candidate has the intellectual skills to successfully practice in a field. These are skills that you should master before you are challenged to demonstrate them!

Case Analysis as Critical Thinking

Case analysis skills are thus important for future careers in general management, consulting, and the professions. These skills are explicitly tested on professional exams and in job interviews. While the basic skill required is systematic, logical thinking, there are techniques that can make this process easier and more productive, particularly when facing either discussion cases or real decision problems in your personal life and career. We will identify and describe these techniques in subsequent Chapters.

Case analysis skills are closely related to critical thinking skills (see Figure 2) and models of rational decision-making. As you develop your skills in case analysis you will be developing critical thinking skills that will become habits of thought that will improve your approach to many of life's problems and opportunities.

Overview of the Book

The remainder of the book is structured as follows. First, I consider the relationship between learning styles and case-based learning. People have different preferences for how they learn and, consequently, there are different ways to approach case-based learning to ensure that you get the most out of it. Second, I provide an overview of a case analysis method. I also provide examples of three other case analysis frameworks. The approach I discuss in depth is not unique; it represents a logical and comprehensive way to approach case analysis. Although the details may vary, every guide to case analysis will have roughly the same structure. With this overview, the core of the book (Chapters 4–7 inclusive) discusses techniques to help you with each step of the case analysis process. Chap-

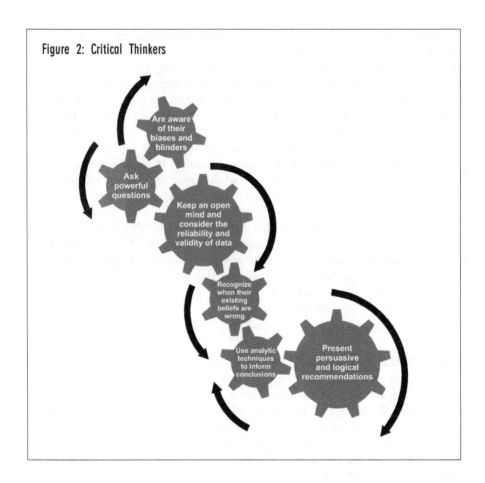

Figure 2: Critical Thinkers

Are aware of their biases and blinders

Ask powerful questions

Keep an open mind and consider the reliability and validity of data

Recognize when their existing beliefs are wrong

Use analytic techniques to inform conclusions

Present persuasive and logical recommendations

ter 8: Working with Others on Case Analyses examines how to effectively work with others on case analyses either in teams assigned to do the analysis or as part of a case discussion in the classroom. Chapter 9: Case-based Examinations provides some guidance for writing case-based examinations either as part of course evaluation procedures or as tests of basic competence used by professional associations to control entry to practice.

Chapter Summary

This Chapter focuses on the reasons cases are used in the classroom and as tests of professional competence and why it is worthwhile for you to develop your case analysis skills. Cases allow instructors to help their students develop critical thinking skills: notably, the abilities to analyze, synthesize and evaluate complex data. These skills are crucial to successful careers as managers or professionals in a variety of fields. Cases provide an opportunity for you to develop these skills without the stress and potential harm of learning on the job. Because cases provide realistic previews of complex and ambiguous decision contexts, many firms and professions use case-based interviews and examinations to test whether you have the skills to enter those fields. Developing your case analysis skills now will help you to get the jobs you aspire to and to succeed in your chosen field.

Problems

1. List and describe the four types of cases discussed in this chapter.

2. List the six learning levels according to Bloom's Hierarchy. Summarize each level.

3. Define and discuss the skills that critical thinkers possess as outlined in this chapter.

Exercises

1. For your intended career path, visit the web site of the professional association or licencing body that controls access to the field and identify any case-based procedures that are used. Look also at previous examination material to see the types of cases used. Refer to this material as you work through this book to see how the techniques could be applied. Some possible occupations to examine include:
   - (a) Accountant/auditor
   - (b) Financial analyst
   - (c) Business valuator
   - (d) Financial planner
   - (e) Management consultant
   - (f) Project manager
   - (g) Information systems designer

2. Go to the web site of the major management consulting firms and navigate to the portion of the web site dealing with interviews. Many of these firms — such as Bain (http://www.joinbain.com/apply-to-bain/interview-preparation/default.asp), Boston Consulting Group (http://www.bcg.com/join_bcg/interview_prep/tips/default.aspx) and McKinsey (http://www.mckinsey.com/Careers/Apply/Interview_tips) — provide video examples of candidates participating in case-based interviews and tips for how to prepare for your interview. Review at least one of these web sites and identify the skills used by candidates and recommended by the companies.

3. Read the JetBlue Case in Appendix B. Prepare an analysis/recommendation for what JetBlue should do (a page or two of bullet points is sufficient for this exercise). We will return to this case

throughout the text to see how the model of case analysis and techniques of case analysis presented later can improve your work.

2 Learning Styles and Case Learning

A common reaction to case-based learning is, "That's not the way I learn!" This is a valid comment; there is a range of learning styles and variation in how comfortable people are with different learning environments. But learning, particularly adult learning that is focused on the higher order categories of Bloom's hierarchy of learning objectives (discussed in Chapter 1) is not a passive activity in which you let your success or failure depend on an accidental fit between the way you learn and the way that life's lessons are structured. You must become self-aware of how you learn best and take steps to engage with learning environments, such as case-based learning in ways that you feel comfortable and will benefit from most. Alternatively, and more challenging but ultimately more rewarding, you need to understand the learning skills that different environments favour and work on developing those skills. Regardless of the strategy you adopt to improving your learning experience, the starting point is to understand your preferences and how they affect your reaction to different learning environments.

This Chapter introduces a model of adult learning that identifies different styles of learning that may reflect your experiences and preferences. These learning styles are then related to different approaches to case analysis that will ensure that, regardless of your learning style, you can successfully use case-based learning and undertake case analyses.

The Kolb Learning Cycle

One of the most influential models of adult learning was developed by Kolb (1984)[1] and modified by Honey and Mumford (2000).[2] He suggested that effective learning involves cycling between different types of activities,

---

[1] Kolb, D.A. (1984). *Experiential Learning*, Englewood Cliffs, NJ.: Prentice Hall.

[2] Honey, P. & Mumford, A. (2000). *The learning styles helper's guide*. Maidenhead: Peter Honey Publications Ltd.

as shown in Figure 3. Since it is a cycle, it is possible to start at various points on this ring. For example, you could start with a concrete experience, take the time to reflect on the experience, develop an abstract conceptualization of the experience (i.e., a lesson that could be generalized to other settings), then try out your knowledge in a new setting. Alternatively you could start by learning a model (abstract conceptualization), experimenting with this model to understand it, see how the model works in practice and then reflect on this experience to suggest how the model could be modified, etc.

Different teaching technologies tend to emphasize different parts of this cycle. For example, writing journals and producing "reaction" essays encourage you to engage in reflective observation; providing laboratory sessions where you duplicate well-known phenomena allows you to have a concrete experience and to experiment with variations; lectures tend to focus on providing theories and frameworks that provide an abstract conceptualization of a field.

Case-based learning is one of the few teaching methods that allow you to experience the complete cycle. A case provides a specific example in which to ground your understanding of a phenomenon. You are encouraged to think about the case and identify what can be learned from this specific example. This may encourage you to develop a theory about what is happening in the case, and/or to draw on other theories to help you conceptualize what is happening. Finally, case analysis is founded on the idea that you must put yourself into the case and, in your mind, think

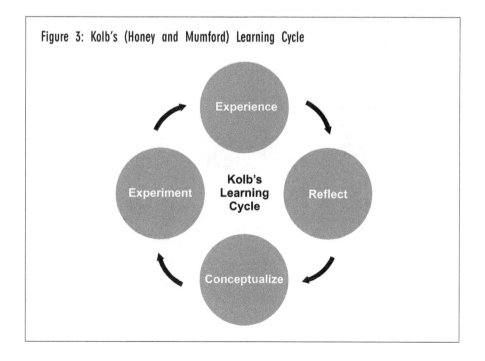

Figure 3: Kolb's (Honey and Mumford) Learning Cycle

through what-if analyses, leading to a recommendation for the decision-maker in the case.

Learning Styles

What may not be obvious is that within this model are different preferences for how you learn new knowledge and how you integrate new knowledge into your view of the world (see Figure 4). First, some people prefer to learn a new topic by exploring examples or gaining hands-on experience; other people prefer to be given a framework or theory when learning a new subject. This is essentially the difference between inductive (bottom up) and deductive (top down) learning. Second, some people de-

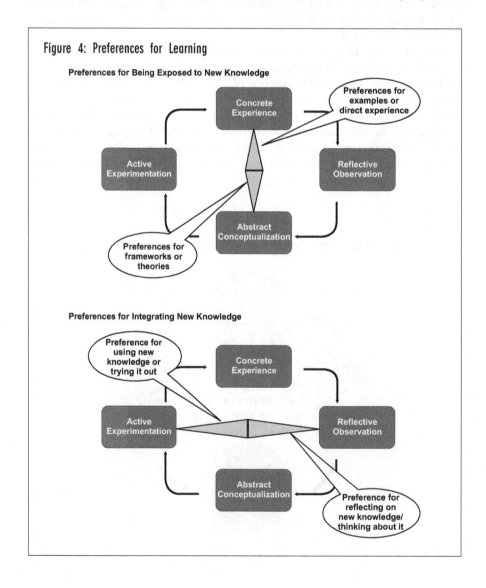

Figure 4: Preferences for Learning

velop their understanding of a topic by reflecting on what they have been shown (i.e., letting it "sink in"); other people prefer to try out new knowledge in different settings to see if they really understand it. These two dimensions can be combined to identify four learning styles.

The learning styles model identifies four types of learners (see Figure 5) — reflectors, theorists, pragmatists, and activists[3] — based on the preferences described above. There is no better or worse way to learn. These different styles can be equally effective, and a person with any of these styles can excel in their chosen field. But recall that Kolb suggests that adults learn best by cycling through four types of learning experiences. This means that your preferred learning style may affect how you approach new knowledge (i.e., where you start on the circle), but not the full range of activities that will lead to successful learning.

Learning Styles and Case Analysis

The discussion above suggests that cases provide a rich setting in which learning may occur, but not all people will approach cases in the same way. The way that you will benefit most from case analysis will depend on

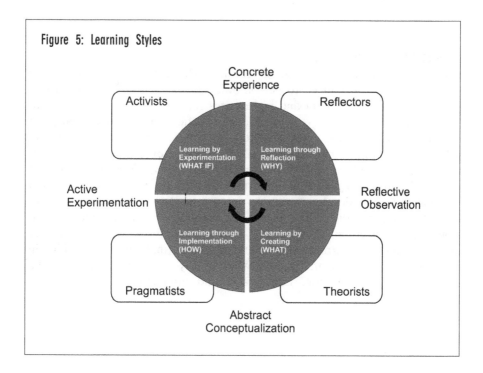

Figure 5: Learning Styles

---

[3] This set of labels is based on Honey, P. & Mumford, A. (2000). *The learning styles helper's guide*. Maidenhead: Peter Honey Publications Ltd. While this is a variant on Kolb's theory, the labels are more helpful than Kolb's categories of converger, assimilator, diverger, accommodator.

your learning style, and you should adapt your approach to case-based learning to ensure that you get all the benefits that are possible from this form of pedagogy. Table 1 suggests some differences in how you approach cases depending on your preferred learning style. In general, using cases in the classroom is coupled with other learning materials that provide analytic techniques and theoretical frameworks. A key difference between learning styles will be the order in which you use these two sets of materials. Reflectors and activists may prefer to read the case first so that they have concrete examples in mind prior to mapping these experiences into theoretical frameworks. Theorists and pragmatists, however, may prefer to understand the tools and frameworks so that they can use these perspectives to make sense of the case material. Developing our understanding of cases will also involve a combination of individual, small group and classroom processes (I will return to this idea in Chapter 8: Working with Others on Case Analyses). People with different learning styles may use these learning opportunities in different ways. It is important to recognize too that your learning style may complement the learning styles of others. The part of the learning cycle that comes easily to you may be a part where others struggle, and vice versa. Finding ways to contribute to the learning of others in groups will add significantly to the quality, productivity and emotional satisfaction of working in groups.

Chapter Summary

Everyone has a preferred style of learning. This may involve preferences for how you are introduced to new knowledge (e.g., through examples versus theoretical frameworks) and preferences for how you reinforce and solidify your learning (e.g., through reflection versus hands-on experimentation). While cases provide a context for learning critical thinking skills and practicing decision-making in complex and ambiguous settings, there are different ways of approaching case analysis that suit your preferred learning styles. It is important for you to understand your own learning style and develop variations in case analysis approaches that ensure that you get the most out of the learning experience and demonstrate your mastery of these crucial skills. While there are no better or worse methods of learning, you should recognize that developing skills in all areas of the Kolb learning cycle will enrich your experience, and make all forms of learning more comfortable and productive.

Table 1: Using Cases across Learning Styles

	Activist	Reflector	Theorist	Pragmatist
Individual reading	Read the case first, develop your own ideas and then read the assigned material.	Read the case first, develop your own ideas and then read the assigned material. Allow long lead time!	Read assigned material first, then read the case. Look for where theory fits/doesn't fit	Read assigned material first, emphasize application of theory in reading the case.
Small group work	Take the lead, explore the case, energize others.	Use the group to deepen understanding, provide feedback.	Use the group to probe theory, brainstorm alternatives.	Use the group to test your ideas, seek implementation issues.
Class discussion	Take the initiative, role play different stakeholders.	Prepare comments in advance, recycle discussion to deeper levels of analysis.	Ask questions, challenge others, offer structure to previous comments.	Role play different stakeholders, focus on takeaways from the discussion.
Most comfortable Kolb cycle stage	Concrete experience.	Reflective observation.	Abstract conceptualization.	Active experimentation.

Problems

1. Outline the four learning styles.

2. Summarize the Kolb Cycle and identify its four components.

3. Why is it beneficial to know our personal learning style when con-
    ducing case analysis? How does this relate to group work?

Exercises

1. Complete the learning styles inventory and determine your pre-
    ferred learning style. Is this consistent with your experiences in dif-
    ferent settings? (An on-line version is available at
    <http://www.brianmac.co.uk/learnstyle.htm> [Dec, 2011], a short
    version is available at <http://rapidbi.com/wpcontent/uploads/
    resourcezone/Learning%20Styles%20Questionnaire.pdf>. The "offi-
    cial version" is available for a fee at http://www.peterhoney.com/).

2. Try an experiment with the next few cases you are assigned. With
    one case try reading the case first following up with the assigned
    technical material; with the next reverse the order in which you ap-
    proach the material. Do you find a difference in your comfort level
    working with the case?

3. Who do you work best with, people who share your learning style
    or people with different styles? Ask your colleagues to complete
    the learning styles inventory and then assess how diversity of learn-
    ing styles in a group affects the richness of the discussion, people's
    comfort levels participating in the group etc.

3 A Model of Case Analysis

Most students initially find case analysis frustrating and difficult (trust me; this feeling will pass as you practice the techniques in this book). It is frustrating because a case does not provide prepackaged information that neatly fits the requirements of the analytical tools we have been trained to use (which is to say they demand that you use more than just knowledge, comprehension and application, i.e.: the lower levels of Bloom's taxonomy, see Figure 1 on page 6). A case will usually include the information that is essential to consider in coming to a recommendation, but it may also include information that is tangential or even misleading. Sometimes the information you need is not included in the case, but is implied by the circumstances. For example, the industry in which a firm operates provides important clues about the business environment and the constraints under which the company operates. Two of the important skills to develop is the ability to identify the information and assumptions that are crucial to your analysis and to separate these data from the "noise" that often accompanies real problems.

Students find case analysis difficult because there is no correct answer. Case analysis is not about applying fixed techniques to arrive at a number or other single solution. In case analysis, and in real life situations, there may not be all the information that you need to implement standard decision models, and the information that is available may include significant uncertainty. This means that you must be flexible in your approach to the case, rather than trying to force the facts of the case into a predetermined model. The lack of a correct answer, however, does not mean there are not better and worse answers. In part the quality of a case analysis is related to the process you follow to analyse the case, and how you communicate this process. A good case analysis write-up will provide evidence that you have applied sound diagnostic skills to the correct information,

This chapter is based on Chapter 3, pp. 25–34 from Richardson, A.J. *Cases in Financial Accounting, 1e* © 2007 Nelson Education Ltd. Reproduced by permission <www.cengage.com/permissions>.

considered a reasonable set of alternatives, and made a reasoned recommendation. (I will return to the issue of how to present a case analysis in Chapter 7: Making Recommendations.) Two people may analyze the same case and come to completely opposite recommendations, yet each could be recognized as having done good work. The purpose of this brief book is to help you understand the case analysis process and to write better case analyses.

In this Chapter I provide an overview of an approach to case analysis that will be elaborated on in the rest of the book. This approach to case analysis represents a particular type of thinking process — as I will discuss further in the next section — that can be learned and mastered through practice.

Case Analysis as a Rational Decision Process

There are many guides to case analysis to which you can refer. Below are three alternatives to which you can compare the approach I will recommend. These examples of case analysis guidelines come from management, public administration and education, respectively. Each of these approaches, regardless of the field to which they were intended to be applied, tends to cover the same ground and will help you develop a sound analysis. Like case analysis itself, the use of any guide to case analysis requires practice and good judgment. Do not apply any guide in a mechanical or checklist manner. Think about what each step is asking you to do and why. Each step contributes towards making a reasoned recommendation based on consideration of a range of alternatives that have the potential to address the specific issues of concern.

The need for guidance in case analysis arises because our normal approach to decision-making is subject to bias. Researchers have identified two systems of decision-making that we use.[1] System 1 is a fast, intuitive and emotional system of thinking that we use every day, most often with great success but occasionally with spectacular failures. In most cases we implement the output of this system (the decision), but we are unaware of how we arrived at that decision. For example, if I ask you what you would like for lunch, or which movie you would like to see, you will probably be able to answer this question quickly, even though implicitly it involves many choices, preferences and constraints that must be balanced. System 1 thinking develops with experience and is hard-wired into people. This system is universal in the sense that everyone will develop heuristics for negotiating their way through life.

System 2 is a slow, methodical and rational process that carefully considers evidence and reaches a preferred course of action. This form of decision-making is conscious, and allows us to reflect on how we make our decisions, and correct those decisions if errors are detected. System 2 is a

[1] See Kahneman, D., and Lane, A. (2011). *Thinking, Fast and Slow.* London: Allen Lane.

rule-based system that can be taught and, therefore, varies among individuals because of their education and cognitive abilities. (Use of this system of thinking thus provides you with a comparative advantage.)

We often like to think that System 2 thinking dominates our approach to life's important decisions, but research shows that System 1 thinking constantly intrudes into our approach to problems, showing up as various biases when compared to rational models (see Appendix A: Decision-Making Biases). For example, our assessment of a problem may be subject to availability bias (our judgment about how likely something is to occur is affected by how easy it is to create a mental image of the event) or anchoring bias (where we look for alternatives or make judgments based on

---

Table 2: Biases Affecting Case Analysis

Common Perceptual and Cognitive Biases

PERCEPTUAL BIASES	BIASES IN EVALUATING EVIDENCE
Exception. We tend to perceive what we expect to perceive. More (unambiguous) information is needed to recognize an unexpected phenomenon.	**Consistency.** Conclusions drawn from a small body of consistent data engender more confidence than ones drawn from a larger body of less consistent data.
Resistance. Perceptions resist change even in the face of new evidence.	**Missing Information.** It is difficult to judge well the potential impact of missing evidence, even if the information gap is known.
Ambiguities. Initial exposure to ambiguous or blurred stimuli interferes with accurate perception, even after more and better information becomes available.	**Discredited Evidence.** Even though evidence supporting a perception may be proved wrong, the perception may not quickly change.
BIASES IN ESTIMATING PROBABILITIES	**BIASES IN PERCEIVING CAUSALITY**
Availability. Probability estimates are influenced by how easily one can imagine an event or recall similar instances.	**Rationality.** Events are seen as part of an orderly causal pattern. Randomness, accident and error tend to be rejected as explanations for observed events. For example, the extent to which other people or countries pursue a coherent, rational, goal-maximizing policy is overestimated.
Anchoring. Probability estimates are adjusted only incrementally in response to new information or further analysis.	
Overconfidence. In translating feelings of certainty into a probability estimate, people are often overconfident, especially if they have considerable expertise.	**Attribution.** Behaviour of others is attributed to some fixed notion of the person or country, while our own behaviour is attributed to the situation in which we find ourselves.

Source: Based on "A Tradecraft Primer: Structured Analytic Techniques for Improving Intelligence Analysis", prepared by the U.S. Government, March 2009. <https://www.cia.gov/library/center-for-the-study-of-intelligence/csi-publications/books-and-monographs/Tradecraft%20Primer-apr09.pdf>

some reference point). Table 2 provides a summary of the main perceptual and cognitive biases that may affect your analysis of cases.

Case analysis guides are a reminder that case analysis should be a rational decision process (System 2 thinking), but it may not be enough to be reminded of this to ensure that your approach to case analysis is unbiased. This book goes beyond providing an overview of the case analysis process by suggesting specific techniques that can help you to overcome our natural cognitive biases.

Below are three overviews of the case analysis process recommended by authors in various fields. Each of these guides provides a System 2 approach to case analysis. Look for the similarities as you read through these examples.

Approaches to Case Analysis: Example 1

Step	Activities
Gaining Familiarity	• Gain an overview of the context • Become comfortable with case details • Reflect on your reaction to case details, characters and events
Recognizing Symptoms	• Identify apparent problems, challenges, obstacles
Identifying Goals	• Identify the goals of each actor in the case • Infer goals where none are stated
Analysis	• Use the context and case details to identify appropriate theory or models • Apply conceptual tools to understand the meaning of facts and symptoms
Diagnosis	• Identify where the goals of actors are not being achieved • Identify where the goals of actors are in conflict • Prioritize which goals should be achieved
Action Planning	• Identify actions that facilitate goal achievement • Evaluate the consequences of implementing those actions, including issues such as cost, timeliness, ethics, etc. • Choose the action to implement • Identify how and by whom the action will be implemented

Source: This table is based on Lundberg, C.C., and Enz. C. (1993). A Framework for Student Case Preparation", *Case Research Journal* N1 N3 (Summer), p. 114.

Approaches to Case Analysis: Example 2

Suggested Tasks in Analyzing Case Studies

Task	Step	Question to Ask
Become familiar with case substance	1	• What are the facts? • What is happening? • Is all relevant information available to you?
Determine central issues	2	• What decisions need to be made? • Who is responsible for making decisions? • What factors, issues, and consequences need to be taken into account?
Identify objectives and goals to be achieved	3	• Which outcomes are possible? • Which are desirable? • Which objectives are most important to whom?
Ascertain resources and constraints	4	• Which forces support and oppose which actions? • Which resources can be marshalled in support of actions? • What are the major obstacles?
Ascertain the nature of conflicts	5	• What is the substance of conflicts? • Can conflicting positions and plans be reconciled?
Identify dynamics of behaviour	6	• Who is exercising leadership? • Are there interpersonal conflicts? • Are the persons involved effective in support of their respective positions?
Determine major alternatives	7	• Are there ideas and strategies that have not been presented? • Is compromise possible? • Are the alternatives complementary, or mutually exclusive?
Assess likely consequences of decisions and actions	8	• What actions are likely to result from the decisions made? • What unintended consequences might emerge? • What are the short and long term consequences for the individuals and the institutions?
Consider appropriate strategies and priorities	9	• What are the most effective ways of achieving and implementing the objectives and decisions? • Are there intermediate steps or stages?
Apply theoretical paradigms and constructs	10	• What are the paradigms and constructs that apply? • What insights are helpful in understanding the situation? Why? • What paradigms do not seem to apply? Why? • How can conflicting concepts be useful, confusing?

Source: McDade, S.A. (1988, 2002, 2011). *Suggested Tasks in Analyzing Case Studies.* Informally published manuscript. Reprinted with permission of author.

Approaches to Case Analysis: Example 3

Finally, a case analysis guide from CaseNex (a professional development company that originated from a research group at the University of Virginia, Curry School of Education, on integrating cases into education programs). The CaseNex model is summarized in Figure 6.

> The steps are:
> 1. identify educational issues, problems, or opportunities as they present themselves in the case;
> 2. recognize different perspectives or values that drive people's actions in the case;
> 3. call up personal, theoretical, and empirical knowledge relevant to the issues identified;
> 4. propose possible actions for handling the issues identified; and
> 5. forecast the likely consequences of such actions.[2]

Figure 6: CaseNex Case Analysis Model

Source: Reproduced from CaseNEX LLC, University of Virginia, Curry School of Education <www.casenex.com>. Reproduced with permission of Casenex, LLC.

---

[2] CaseNEX LLC, University of Virginia, Curry School of Education <www.casenex.com>. Reproduced with permission of Casenex, LLC.

The point of these three examples is that case analysis is primarily about being logical and disciplined in your approach to analyzing decision problems. It is not about mechanically applying formulae to get a correct answer. There are variations in how people recommend going about case analysis, but all will try to lead you through a basic linear logic from facts, through issues and alternatives, to recommendations for action. The model below should be taken in this light, and used in a context sensitive and creative way to generate good case analyses.

A Model of Case Analysis

To help you think about case analysis, I have broken down the process into the following stages:

1. information gathering;
2. issue identification;
3. issue prioritization;
4. alternative generation;
5. evaluation of alternatives;
6. recommendation; and
7. implementation issues.

The case analysis process I recommend and will illustrate throughout the rest of this book is summarized in Figure 7. The first three stages make sure that you have correctly identified the problem or opportunity (this

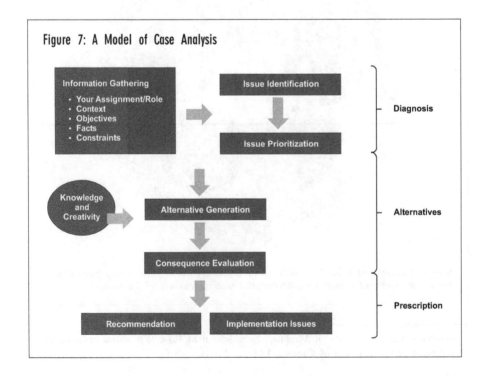

Figure 7: A Model of Case Analysis

will be referred to as an "issue" from here on) in the case (diagnosis). The next two stages lead you through the process of developing possible courses of action to deal with the problem or exploit the opportunity (alternatives). The final two stages identify the preferred course of action and ensure that you have thought through the implications of implementing the preferred course of action (prescription).

I will elaborate on each of these stages below. Once you have a road map of the process we will examine specific techniques that can help you deal with each stage of the journey in subsequent Chapters.

Information Gathering

The first stage in any case analysis is straightforward: read the case. In fact, you may need to read the case several times. In the rest of this guide you will learn what to look for as you read. In brief, you are reading to understand your role in completing the case analysis and to identify the key facts, the issues, the users of the information and their objectives, and any factors that may limit the range of alternatives that can be considered. Rosen summarized what to look for as you read a case as the following mantra: facts, objectives, constraints.[3] You should read the case at least three times: first, to understand the facts (an overview); second, to identify objectives and constraints (reading between the lines to identify the objectives of key decision makers and constraints on potential solutions that may not be explicit); finally, to test your hypotheses about what to do against case facts.

Understand your Assignment

One of the most important parts of the case to understand is the "required" assignment (sometimes referred to as the case "rubric"). Most case analyses specifically ask you to prepare your analysis from the perspective of a person in a particular role communicating to a particular person using a particular reporting format. This is typically, but not always, found in the final sentence or paragraph of the case. For example, you may be asked to assume the role of a staff accountant preparing a memo for the senior management of a public company, or you may be asked to provide a report to an audit partner from the perspective of an audit manager working on a private-company audit of financial statements to be submitted to a bank to support a loan application. The "required" part of the case is important because it provides the terms of reference for your assignment and, most important, identifies the "client" you are serving. A key requirement of any recommendation that you make is that it satisfies the objectives of the client.

An important part of the "requirements" of case analysis is to determine what type of decision is being made in the case (see Figure 8). In

---

[3] Rosen, L.S. (1982). *Financial Accounting: A Canadian Casebook*. Toronto: Prentice-Hall.

some cases the analysis requires a strategic perspective and it is appropriate to suggest major changes to the business model. These are decisions usually made at the level of the Board of Directors and C-suite (CEO, CFO, COO etc.). In cases dealing with functional levels of the organization (c.g., marketing, accounting etc.), the strategy of the organization must be taken as a constraint and the decision-maker is concerned with tactical decisions about how to implement the strategy. Rarely a case will deal with operational issues, which are the day-to-day decisions needed to implement the chosen tactics.

Understand the Context

As part of your first reading of the case, identify any aspects of the business and its environment that may affect the organization. For example, identify the industry in which the company operates, and any special regulations or laws that may apply. (N.B. this may not be an explicit part of the case and will require that you do some research into the industry.) Determine whether the company is in good financial condition or in crisis. Identify who will use the analysis and what decisions will be affected. Identify management's motives and incentives to make choices in a particular way and try to assess whether the information management is working with is reliable. (For example, with regard to financial information, in large companies this may be a question of the quality of the internal control system — that is, the steps management has taken to ensure the reliability of the information on which it bases the financial statements and performance reports; in smaller companies it may simply be a question of the competence of the managers making the key assumptions required by the financial reporting system.) It is crucial to separate reliable information from opinion in the case.

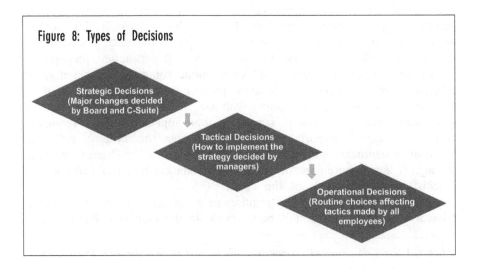

Figure 8: Types of Decisions

Strategic Decisions
(Major changes decided
by Board and C-Suite)

Tactical Decisions
(How to implement the
strategy decided by
managers)

Operational Decisions
(Routine choices affecting
tactics made by all
employees)

Discussing the case with others may help you identify important contextual factors. Based on our personal experiences, exposure to different businesses and our own reading of the business press, each of us develops a store of tacit knowledge about how the world works. When you discuss cases in groups, you become aware that you have tacit knowledge that you can use to educate your peers (as will they) and enrich your own analyses of cases. Don't be afraid to use this knowledge in your analyses; however, you may want to verify that what you "know" is valid. (Remember that our knowledge is subject to cognitive biases.) You may not be able to identify all of the important contextual variables initially, but with practice your skill at this will improve.

If the case is based on a real company or on a specific industry, it is fair for you to read about the company and industry to get a better understanding of the context. The purpose of the case is to immerse you in the context that the decision-makers faced, so more information is better. The only danger is hindsight bias. When we know what happened, it is easy to reinterpret facts or to make recommendations based on the certainty of known outcomes. Your recommendation, however, must be based on what was known at the time and the facts provided in the case.

Identify Important Case Facts

Too often, students analyzing a case waste their time (and the time of the person reading the analysis) by repeating the facts of the case. Your analysis need only mention those facts that are relevant. Imagine that you and a friend are crossing a road and your friend is about to step off the curb in front of a car. What do you call out? Most likely you yell something short and forceful that will trigger the response that will save your friend's life, like "Car!" You probably don't yell: "Look! A black two-door late model sedan!" The key fact in this situation is the existence of the car because of the danger it poses to your friend's life. If, on the other hand, you and your friend were on a car dealer's lot looking for a particular type of car to buy, calling out the colour and style of the car would be relevant to the decision being made.

Any time case facts are mentioned in your case write-up, they should move your analysis forward. The important facts are the ones that help you identify issues and evaluate alternatives. Do not just repeat case facts in your analysis — tell the reader why those facts are important to your analysis.[4] If you have restated a case fact, ask yourself: "Why is this piece of information important to me? How does it affect my thinking about this company?" The most effective way to identify which case facts are important is to have a model or framework to guide your analysis. Part of your instructor's role is to provide you with these frameworks, which you will practise using by applying them to cases. These frameworks may in-

---

[4] It is common to distinguish between data, information, knowledge and wisdom (e.g., Rowley, Jennifer (2007).

clude tools for quantitative analysis. For example, the case might concern short-term cash flow problems. One way to identify such issues is to calculate financial statement ratios, such as the quick ratio [(Current assets — Inventory)/Current liabilities]. The purpose of such frameworks is to help you identify — and, in some cases, create through calculations — the key data on which to base your analysis.

Issue Identification

Most cases focus on a particular issue or set of issues. The term "issue" is used generically to refer to both threats and opportunities facing an organization. When reading the case, keep a list of all of the issues you come across. In a business, issues are circumstances where there is a gap between what is desired or expected and what occurred, and where management must make choices regarding how to deal with the issue. Those choices will have a material impact on the welfare of any stakeholder. It is important to use your own judgment when reading the issues identified by the characters in the case. It is not uncommon for people engulfed in problems to be unable to see the key issues clearly; your role is to provide an objective overview of the case. Chapter 4: Identifying Issues provides some techniques for this step.

Issue Prioritization

You will probably encounter multiple issues in the case. Not all issues are equally important. It may not be crucial for you to spend a lot of time on some of the issues. The key is to prioritize them — that is, list them in order of importance. The importance of various issues depends on the objectives of the decision maker in the case and the consequences of the issues. Obviously, any issue that could affect the survival of the firm is central. An issue that is short-term and is likely to resolve itself is probably not worth acting on.

Be careful also to differentiate between symptoms and root causes. To diagnose issues successfully, you must be able to look beyond the symptoms to see what is causing the problem. For example, a company may be experiencing cash shortages and high turnover. A consultant who suggests a bank loan and employee recognition awards, but who misses the company's too rapid expansion and overworked key personnel, will not be helping the firm survive. The case may suggest that a key issue is how to disclose some financial transaction, but on analysis you may conclude that the company has not measured the transaction correctly, or you may conclude that the transaction has been not been recognized properly. Before trying to provide a solution, be sure you understand the issue. Chapter 4: Identifying Issues provides techniques to help with this aspect of your analysis.

Alternative Generation

Once the issues have been identified you must develop a plan of action. There will be multiple ways of handling each issue. You should be able to identify the key characteristics of each alternative — for example, how difficult or costly it would be to implement, how many of the issues in the case it would address, and what conflicts it might generate. Be sensitive to solutions that are mutually exclusive or mutually supportive. Some steps would have to be taken at the same time in order for both to succeed; sometimes the opposite is true — taking two steps at the same time would negate both.

This is the part of case analysis where you can apply your creativity and knowledge. Your knowledge provides you with a set of possible responses; your creativity helps you recognize new applications for existing responses, potential variations on standard responses that would best fit the situation, and novel ways of addressing issues. Chapter 5: Identifying Alternatives provides specific techniques to generate these kinds of alternatives.

One of the most serious blunders a case analyst can make is to jump immediately to a recommendation as "obvious" or "the only course of action possible" without exercising some creativity first. This is sometimes referred to as "ready, fire, aim." You want to slow down before you pull the trigger and make sure you have the correct target in your sights. Be careful, too, not to create "straw men" among your alternatives (defined in Figure 9). Straw men in this context are alternatives developed for the sole purpose of rejecting them. A person reading your analysis should be able to see that the alternatives you have considered are reasonable and reasonably comprehensive. If your alternatives are not well thought out, why should we believe your recommendation is?

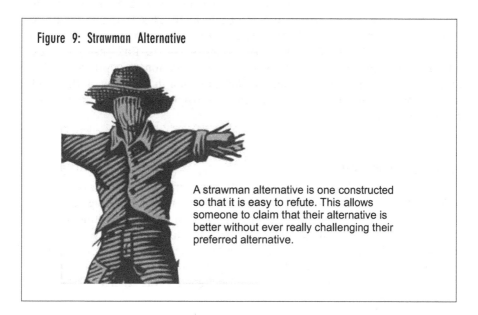

Figure 9: Strawman Alternative

A strawman alternative is one constructed so that it is easy to refute. This allows someone to claim that their alternative is better without ever really challenging their preferred alternative.

Evaluate Consequences

Once you have a list of alternatives, you must narrow the list down to one recommendation. To do this you must compare the consequences of each alternative and determine which one best meets the objectives of the decision maker. It is important at this point to consider both quantitative and qualitative outcomes. For example, strategic considerations sometimes require that the alternative with the best short-term financial outcome be rejected. It will be helpful at this stage to develop a set of criteria, based on the decision maker's objectives, to use in evaluating each alternative.

At this stage you may find there is no clear winner among your alternatives. Each of the alternatives may address a subset of the issues or have different cost/benefit tradeoffs. You may need to return to your earlier analysis and refine your identification of the objectives of your assignment or of the importance of various issues to ensure that you can identify the best alternative. You may also need to rethink your alternatives, and ensure that you have been creative in considering what could be done. This is where "thinking outside the box" becomes valuable. Chapter 6: Evaluating Alternatives will provide you with techniques to ensure that the right alternatives are brought forward.

Recommendation

Once you have decided on the best alternative, you must present your recommendation to the decision maker. Your recommendation must be fully justified in terms of that person's objectives and capabilities. For example, if the company is a family business and the problem in the case is the incompetence of the controller (who is also the president's nephew), your recommendation must be sensitive to this detail.

Your recommendation should make a convincing case for implementation based on the analysis you have performed. This is not the time to add additional reasons or details! The recommendation is a summary of your analysis, not another step in the analysis. If you find that you must introduce new material to justify your recommendation, you probably need to go back to your analysis, and make sure you have done a thorough job. Chapter 7: Making Recommendations provides guidance on communicating your case analysis.

Implementation Issues

Finally, you should consider how your recommendation will be implemented. In part you will have considered this issue in deciding which alternative to recommend, but depending on the case requirements, you may need to specify what will need to be done to implement your recommendation. This may involve, for example, indicating the order in which your recommendations should be implemented, or what additional work — such as consultation with various parties or changes in operations — may be necessary to ensure success.

Chapter Summary

The case analysis process is a logical and systematic method for dealing with complex and ambiguous problems. It involves a careful reading of the case to establish the facts, identifying and prioritizing the issues that a decision-maker would have to address in this setting, generating a rich set of alternatives that address the issues, evaluating these alternatives according to the objectives of the decision-maker and, finally, making a recommendation for action (taking into account implementation issues as appropriate). Although the overall logic should be common-sense, it requires self-discipline to implement these guidelines and sensitivity to the case details to vary from the basic model when necessary. It is also important to recall that we all suffer from cognitive biases that may affect decisions without our being aware of their effect. The techniques described in the rest of the book focus, in particular, on ensuring that your use of the case analysis method is not side-tracked by these biases.

Problems

1. Describe and compare the two main systems we use for decision making.

2. Explain some of the main biases that affect case analysis.

3. Describe the steps involved in the approach to case analysis recommended in this book.

4. Define "issue" as it applies to case analysis.

Exercises

1. Identify at least one other framework or guideline for case analysis. Compare the categories used across this additional framework and the one recommended in this chapter. Identify the common elements across these frameworks.

2. The model provided in this Chapter is a guide, not a set of rules. Examine the next few cases you analyze, and identify where some of the steps were treated briefly while others were elaborated. Can you identify the circumstances in which the basic logic outlined in this Chapter is modified?

3. Look up the "scientific method." How does the normative model of science reflected in the "scientific method" relate to the model of case analysis presented in this Chapter?

4. Read the "JetBlue" case in Appendix B: JetBlue Airways' Customer Service Fiasco. Prepare a case analysis based on the model in this Chapter. You will be asked to return to this case as we move through the book to see how different techniques can aid your analysis of this case.

4 Identifying Issues

> "If I had an hour to solve a problem and my life depended on the solution, I would spend the first 55 minutes determining the proper question to ask, for once I know the proper question, I could solve the problem in less than 5 minutes".
>
> — Albert Einstein

Cases are usually written because something interesting or unusual has happened. This may be something negative, such as a major fraud, environmental disaster or loss of a major customer. It may be something positive such as rapid growth of the company, entry into new markets or the decision to make an initial public offering of equity. In other words, the case focuses on either a problem or opportunity that a decision-maker in the case must address, or it asks you to evaluate the decision that was made. The case writer tries to provide the reader with a rich description of the conditions surrounding the event in order to allow the case analyst to put themselves into the shoes of the decision-maker. The event that attracted the interest of the case writer, however, is typically just a symptom of the real issues. For example, the U.S. landing of men on the moon in 1969 was a significant event in U.S. history, and it would be reasonable to write a case about this event, but a case analyst must understand the event as a reaction to the U.S.S.R.'s launch of the first satellite (Sputnik) in 1957 in the context of the Cold War between communist and capitalist countries following WWII. If one asked why man went to the moon, focusing on the event itself would miss the issue of earth-bound politics.

As a continuing example, I will refer to the case of JetBlue (see Appendix B: JetBlue Airways' Customer Service Fiasco), which suffered a severe blow to its reputation due to its handling of the effects on its operations of a major snow storm in 2007. A notable incident was the case of passengers who were kept in a plane on a runway waiting to takeoff for nearly 11 hours. In order to advise the company on what it should do when faced with this event, it is crucial to ensure that the right issues are identified.

This Chapter reviews approaches to the identification of issues that ensure that you push past easily identified but superficial symptoms to the real issues that you must address in your analysis, and how to prioritize these issues for action.

Gap Analysis

Issues in case analysis arise primarily because there is a gap between what is currently happening and what we would like to happen or what stakeholders expected to happen. In order to understand what the issues are in the case, we must therefore develop a basic sense of the objectives of stakeholders and decision-makers. I will return to this issue in Chapter 6: Evaluating Alternatives, but for now it is enough to have a high-level view of these objectives/expectations.

There are two approaches to developing expectations against which actual events can be compared. First, we can identify actual objectives or expectations stated in the case. Second, we can identify normative models that provide expectations for what "should" happen based either on rational models of behaviour or on enforceable social norms (e.g., codes of governance conduct).

In your reading of the case, one of the things that you should be looking for is a statement about the objectives of the company. If this is not explicit in the case, and the case deals with a real company, then some research may identify the company's overall objectives. For example, most companies will have a "vision statement" that provides a sense of the preferred future for the company. If this vision statement has been constructed according to best practices, it should reflect the objectives of key stakeholders and the strategic direction management intends to follow in achieving those objectives. For example, Heinz has the following vision statement: "As the trusted leader in nutrition and wellness, Heinz — the original Pure Food Company — is dedicated to the sustainable health of people, the planet and our Company." Google's vision statement is: "to organize the world's information and make it universally accessible and useful."[1] For these companies, therefore, an issue would be any event that impedes achievement of their vision or provides an opportunity to attain it.

It may also be possible that the case provides direct evidence on: (1) what the company is trying to achieve that can provide a baseline for identifying the gap between current conditions and what was expected, and (2) what various stakeholders have experienced compared to their expectations of the company. For example, the case may provide evidence of dissatisfaction expressed by a stakeholder group about events: managers

---

[1] "Google's Vision Statement" From <http://www.google.com/about/corporate/company/index.html> Accessed April 19, 2013.

may identify opportunities that are not yet being exploited, customers may express interest in new products or dissatisfaction with service or products already received, and various interest groups may be monitoring organizational performance and raising concerns. These types of data indicate that a gap of some form is present in the case, and identify issues that should be explored.

In some cases, our gap analysis will be based on a normative model of performance rather than something that the company itself has specified. You should use appropriate models from your professional education for this purpose. For example, there are models of corporate governance (e.g., Sarbanes-Oxley), inventory planning and production scheduling, stakeholder management and other aspects of organizational functioning that could be drawn on as the case requires highlighting where issues exist in the case.

One approach to gap analysis is based on McKinsey's 7S model, shown in Figure 10. The 7S model suggests that optimum functioning of an organization requires alignment of 7 aspects of the organization: shared values, strategy, structure, style (or culture), skills, systems and staff. This model is used in two ways. First, we can use it as a tool to identify issues by locating the events in the case within this framework. For example, in the JetBlue case, did the problem in handling the snow storm arise because our strategy was not aligned with our structure, or the staff available, or the systems in place? Second, we can use this model to identify alternatives by examining the current state of the organization on these dimensions and identifying how these dimensions must change to achieve

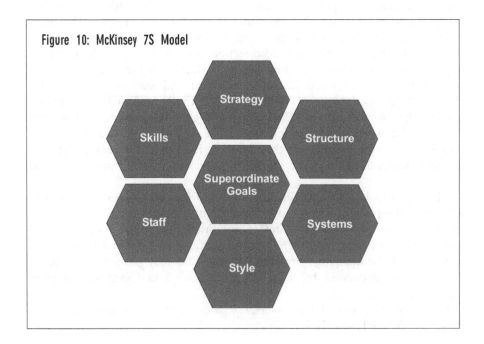

Figure 10: McKinsey 7S Model

Strategy

Skills

Structure

Superordinate Goals

Staff

Systems

Style

the vision of the organization held by key decision-makers. Approaches to generating alternatives are considered in the next Chapter.

Gap analysis helps us to identify where expectations or aspirations have not been met. Gap analysis by itself, however, may not tell us what issues gave rise to the unmet expectations. The techniques below help us to identify these issues.

Root Cause Analysis

The key to identifying the right issues is to differentiate between symptoms and causes. For example, while the plight of the people stuck on JetBlue's plane for 11 hours waiting for clearance to takeoff is of concern (they had boarded expecting a short commuter flight, and during their time waiting for takeoff they ran out of food and water, and the restrooms ceased to function), it is likely that it is a symptom of something deeper. If our analysis stops at the symptom, then the solution to JetBlue's situation might be as simple as apologizing and compensating passengers for the delay. It would perhaps also be inappropriate to stop our analysis of the JetBlue case by saying that the storm was a once-in-a-millennium event that would never be repeated, and so nothing can be done. If this was a completely unique situation, then little could be learned from it by management; but if this is the symptom of other problems over which management has control then it is likely that the problem would reoccur, and it is likely that future passengers would avoid the airline. The distinction between cause and symptom has been developed into a set of techniques called "root cause analysis" that attempt to systematically move from the presenting symptoms to the root cause of the problem. These root causes are the issues that should be identified and dealt with in case analysis (See Figure 11).

Root cause analysis refers to a set of techniques most of which have been developed to diagnose mechanical/electronic systems or quality issues. I describe two techniques that have the most potential for helping identify issues in case analysis: fishbone diagrams and the five why technique.

Fishbone Diagrams

Fishbone diagrams are a graphic representation of a thought process that traces symptoms back through the areas that may have given rise to the symptom. The diagram looks like the spine of a fish (see Figure 12) hence the name. The "ribs" of the diagram are the major categories of factors that could have caused the "event" or "effect." Typically these factors include people, processes, equipment, materials, environment and management, as shown in the Figure. Sometimes authors will use mnemonics to help people remember the categories and rephrase these categories with a common first letter, such as methods, machinery, management, materials and manpower, or the components of McKinsey's 7S model. The actual categories used should reflect your judgement about

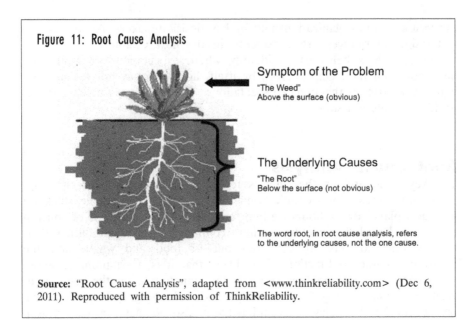

Figure 11: Root Cause Analysis

Source: "Root Cause Analysis", adapted from <www.thinkreliability.com> (Dec 6, 2011). Reproduced with permission of ThinkReliability.

the important factors in your case. The generic categories listed may provide a starting point for your own analysis of important factors in your case.

For each category of causal factor, your analysis should indicate how, if at all, this factor contributed to the observed symptom. For example, in Jetblue the decision to keep people on the aircraft related to a company policy to always get people to their destination rather than cancelling

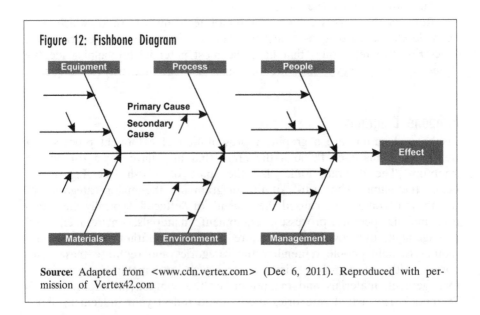

Figure 12: Fishbone Diagram

Source: Adapted from <www.cdn.vertex.com> (Dec 6, 2011). Reproduced with permission of Vertex42.com

flights, and to the lack of personnel with authority on site to override this policy. Pushing this analysis further to secondary causes, you might observe that the company policy is part of their attempt to differentiate themselves from larger airlines and the lack of personnel on site reflects a lean operating strategy. In other words, the event was a consequence of the company's competitive strategy interacting with unusual weather conditions. This identification of the issue leads us to a different set of responses than just focusing on the symptom itself.

The key analytic contribution of the fishbone diagram is to encourage you to systematically consider the role of key factors in any event. The diagram also encourages you to go beyond the immediate causes to identify causes of causes (secondary causes): which raises the question, how far should you go in seeking causes? The five why method provides an answer to this question.

The Five Why Method

There is a famous nursery rhyme that provides a cautionary tale of causal links from small events to major consequences.[2] This rhyme captures the logic behind the "five why" method of root cause analysis. It is probably coincidence that this rhyme has five steps!

> For want of a nail the shoe was lost.
> For want of a shoe the horse was lost.
> For want of a horse the rider was lost.
> For want of a rider the battle was lost.
> For want of a battle the kingdom was lost.
> And all for the want of a horseshoe nail.

The five why method suggests that for most events asking "why" five times is enough to take us to the root cause of an event. The five why method would reverse the order of lines in the nursery rhyme and begin by asking: why was the kingdom lost? Each "why" brings us closer to the original cause of the kingdom being lost.

Asking questions is, of course, the key to gaining knowledge. It is important that you "interrogate" the case material to understand it. Rudyard Kipling (Just So Stories, 1902) wrote:

> I keep six honest serving-men
> (They taught me all I knew);
> Their names are What and Why and When
> And How and Where and Who.

These basic questions can tell you much about the situation in the case, but of all the possible questions that you could ask, "why" is the most important. The "why" question forces us to look for causal relationships and for the mechanisms that generate the events in the case. The "why" question allows us to probe below the surface facts (things like: when, who, where) to understand the deeper structure of the case. The "why" question opens up other questions since, typically, each "why" will draw attention to other

---

[2] <http://www.rhymes.org.uk/for_want_of_a_nail.htm> provides a history of this rhyme.

causal paths and factors that need to be taken into account. The "why" question is also the most likely to lead us to think about the issues in a manner that will generate insights that can be used to correct a problem or seize an opportunity. It is likely that the case writer has provided you with the answers to the "easy" questions. The basic facts of the case will be laid out for you to see who did what, when and where. The "why" of the case, however, is less likely to be as obvious and this is where your analysis adds value. The pyramid in Figure 13 captures the relationships between questions and the power of those questions in case analysis. Make sure that you are asking powerful questions as you explore the case.

To return to the JetBlue case, we might ask a series of questions as follows:

- Event: JetBlue passengers were trapped on a plane for 11 hours. **Why?**
- Because an unprecedented snowstorm prevented takeoff, and they were waiting for clearance to leave. **Why?**
  o Because JetBlue promised passengers never to cancel a flight, and to get them to their destination (even if a little late). **Why?**
    □ Because JetBlue is a new small carrier who differentiated themselves from major air carriers by offering low cost and high customer service. **Why?**
  o Because Jetblue did not have the operational flexibility to respond to the unusual circumstances by changing their routines. **Why?**
    □ Because JetBlue had never experienced or anticipated this type of event, and was operating with minimal staff. **Why?**

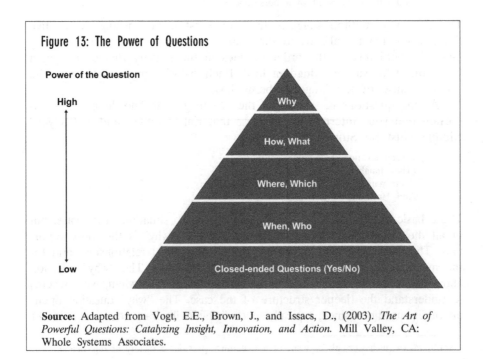

Figure 13: The Power of Questions

Power of the Question

High

Why

How, What

Where, Which

When, Who

Closed-ended Questions (Yes/No)

Low

Source: Adapted from Vogt, E.E., Brown, J., and Issacs, D., (2003). *The Art of Powerful Questions: Catalyzing Insight, Innovation, and Action.* Mill Valley, CA: Whole Systems Associates.

In the set of questions above note that there may be more than one reason something happened. In this case, the five why technique follows each branch of the answer to ensure that root causes are identified.

The five why method, combined with the fishbone diagram, provides a way of systematically exploring the contribution of each major factor to an observed outcome. These factors are each potentially an "issue" that needs to be addressed to prevent reoccurrence of the event or to prepare the company to better deal with the circumstances described.

Technical Analysis and Identifying Issues

The use of root cause analysis and the five why method is an attempt to direct your attention to various issues in the case. These are generic techniques that can be applied to any form of case analysis. Every functional area in business, however, has also developed its own techniques for identifying issues. The sections above complement these approaches. So, for example, if your analysis suggests that there are liquidity or solvency issues facing the firm and the case provides you with financial data (or these data are available from other sources), then you will want to do appropriate technical analyses as a way of both justifying your identification of the issue, suggesting how important the issue is to the company (see the next section for further commentary on prioritizing issues), and providing input to the selection of alternatives for dealing with the issue. If the company faces a key strategic choice, then using SWOT analysis (strengths, weakness, opportunities threats), PEST analysis (political, economic, social and technological) or Porter's five-forces model (threat of new competition, threat of substitute products or services, bargaining power of customers, bargaining power of suppliers, intensity of competitive rivalry) may provide appropriate insights into the issues facing the organization.

Nothing is this book takes away from the importance of doing sound technical analysis of the facts of the case. Recall from the discussion in Chapter 3 that some of the case "facts" must be constructed based on the raw data in the case. The technical analysis techniques you have been provided with in your professional education are ways of changing data into information.

If used conscientiously, the combination of technical analysis and root cause analysis methods could generate a large number of potential issues; but which issues are really worth addressing? This leads to the need to prioritize issues.

Prioritizing Issues

The issues that we should address in our analysis are those that are significant to the company, its stakeholders and decision-makers, and are likely to reoccur. One technique for visualizing this relationship is the risk matrix. It is also useful at this stage to reduce the number of issues to a reasonable set. If consideration of the risk and consequences of the issues is not enough to accomplish this, then affinity diagrams may be used to identify higher order groupings of issues that would be appropriate for further analysis.

Risk Matrix

One technique for capturing the importance of issues is to consider the impact or severity of its consequences, the frequency with which it might occur, and the probability of it doing so. The risk matrix (see Figure 14) is a qualitative approach to picturing this relationship. For each issue identified consider the consequences to the organization. Any issue that could threaten the survival of the organization or affect the health and safety of any stakeholder would likely be categorized as having severe consequences. An issue that is self-correcting or a nuisance, rather than a threat to survival, would be considered to have insignificant or marginal consequences. The likelihood of the issue generating an event ranges from the highly improbable (rare) to almost certain. Note that even rare events with severe consequences and minor events that occur with certainty may be worth further consideration within this framework.

Although the risk matrix is based on subjective scales of severity and frequency, your input to this type of model should be as detailed and well

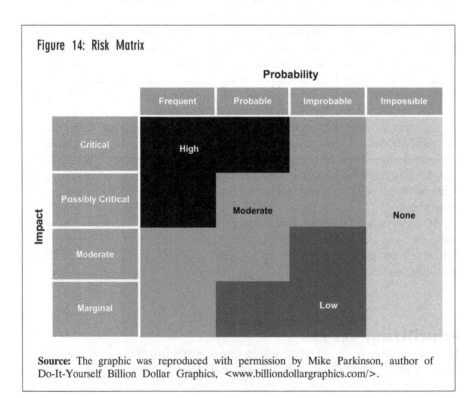

Figure 14: Risk Matrix

Source: The graphic was reproduced with permission by Mike Parkinson, author of Do-It-Yourself Billion Dollar Graphics, <www.billiondollargraphics.com/>.

documented as possible. This will allow you to audit your analysis and recommendations, as recommended in Chapter 7: Making Recommendations. For example, for each issue you should be able to specify what types of consequences may arise (e.g., financial, legal, ethical, etc.), how large the cost will be and who will bear these costs (at least initially: lawsuits and insurance may change where the cost ultimately is borne). For example, in JetBlue's case the snow storm created many immediate problems for passengers in-flight at that time, such as lost luggage and delays in reaching their destination, but the greatest cost of the event was probably reputational. High visibility events, like keeping passengers in a plane on the runway for 11 hours, can result in potential customers avoiding the airline and current customers reducing their loyalty. This would have severe consequences for the company's future revenues. In fact, immediately after the event, JetBlue undertook surveys of both customers and non-customers to gauge how JetBlue's reputation had been impacted.

Similarly, the frequency of occurrence of an issue or event should be based on either historical data or an assessment of the process that generated the issue in the first place. For example, in JetBlue's case, how often do major airports get shut down by weather or other disruptions? During past closures, how long did they last? Perhaps, if JetBlue's problem was caused by a one-in-a-hundred-year storm, then it may not be worth changing practices at the airline. In principle, the frequency of such events can be estimated based on weather statistics or data from the airport itself.

The discussion above suggests that the issue of keeping passengers onboard a plane during a weather event would be a low frequency, high consequence event. Most risk matrices would classify this as an issue of moderate importance that should be addressed. [It should be noted that JetBlue faced another incident of passengers being trapped on board a plane (this time for seven hours) in October 2011.[3]]

The risk matrix is a more sophisticated version of Pareto Analysis (also known as the 80:20 rule). This approach recognizes that the majority (80%) of costs and/or benefits in any particular situation are caused by a small portion (20%) of events or issues. So the process of prioritization focuses on identifying those few events/issues (the 20%) that create the largest impact. These would be the issues that fall into "high" risk category in Figure 15. (The high risk category is assigned to 3 out of 16 cells in this matrix, or 18.75% of cases.)

Affinity Diagrams

The number of issues that should be carried forward into the next stages of analysis will depend on the details of the case being analyzed; but generally issues will be clustered (e.g., within one spine of the fishbone dia-

---

[3] Popken, B. "JetBlue Giving Refunds To Customers Trapped For 7 Hours On Tarmac", *The Consumerist.* Oct 31, 2011. <http://consumerist.com/2011/10/ jetblue-giving-refunds-to-customers-trapped-for-7-hours-on-tarmac.html>

gram), or may be subsumed under a broader category that allows you to identify an "issue area."[4] For example, in the JetBlue case issues concerning operational policies, personnel competencies and emergency preparedness might be considered as separate issues or recognized as part of an issue with contingency planning. Affinity diagrams are a technique used to help reduce the overall number of issues to a manageable set. A common approach to this task is to write each identified issue on a post-it note and to display all of the issues on a surface.[5] The notes are then rearranged to bring together those issues that seem to be related until a structure emerges that reduces the total number of issues to a reasonable number (a heuristic is to identify a maximum of three to five issue areas). After the intuitive relationship between issues has been identified, it is then necessary to analyze the set of issues and deduce the common, higher order issue that binds them together. These higher level issues will be the ones that are carried forward for decision-making.

In the JetBlue case, for example, the wide range of issues experienced might be summarized into two main issues: how to repair the brand name of JetBlue after such an incident and how to manage the operational risks associated with a small, lean air carrier. The more detailed issues that might be combined into these categories are shown below.

- Brand risks [Customer Perception/Experience]
  - Past customers (make amends)
  - Current customers (maintain brand loyalty)
  - Future customers (reinforce the value proposition)

- Operational risks
  - Strategy (do our commitments create risks)
  - Systems (do our systems allow us to respond to problems)
  - Cost (can we remain a low cost carrier and deal with the other issues).

Chapter Summary

A key stage in the case analysis process is identifying issues. Issues are challenges, opportunities or problems that a decision-maker must address. Issues often appear at the end of long causal chains; the presenting issue, or symptom, may not be the issue that requires the decision-maker's attention. This Chapter illustrates how root cause analysis and the "five why" method can be used to ensure that your analysis pushes beyond the symptom to find the deeper issues that must be addressed. These techniques may generate a long list of issues but the decision-maker's time and cognitive capacity are limited so it is also necessary to prioritize is-

---

[4] The term *issue area* is commonly used in political science to denote a broad policy area in which multiple interconnected issues may occur (such as climate change or financial stability).

[5] A somewhat more sophisticated version of this method is reflected in concept mapping. There is software available to help implement this technique.

sues and/or to aggregate issues into broad categories that provide an "issue area" in need of attention. The use of risk matrices and affinity diagrams help to ensure that the issues that will focus the rest of your case analysis are the most important ones for the decision-maker to deal with.

Problems

1. Differentiate between the "symptoms" and the "root causes" of issues in cases. Which should you focus on when conducting case analysis? Why?

2. Which of the six basic questions (how, when, why, what, where, who) is the most important to ask in case analysis? Explain what this question helps us achieve.

3. Describe the criteria by which you should prioritize issues.

Exercises

1. During 2008/2009 the world economy experienced a significant economic decline that has been compared to the Great Depression in severity and scope.
   (a) Review the press reports from this period and identify as many issues as possible (e.g., stock market decline, threat of deflation, banking illiquidity, unemployment, political unrest etc.). Use the risk matrix and affinity diagrams to help focus your attention on the key issues.
   (b) Review the press reports from this period and identify as many government responses to the crisis as you can. What issues was each response meant to address?
   (c) Based on a comparison of your views in (a) and (b), did government decision-makers focus on the right issues?

2. Refer to Appendix C: Eisner's Mousetrap (Disney).
   (a) Prepare a fishbone diagram for this case.
   (b) Group the issues identified into a small number of core issues (use the affinity diagram method).
   (c) Prioritize the issues you have identified. Explain the data and method you used to prioritize the issues.

3. Every discipline has its own techniques that can support case analysis. For your own field, identify qualitative and quantitative techniques that can be used to (a) recognize problems and opportunities facing organizations and (b) prioritize issues (i.e., identifying the magnitude of risks and opportunities).

5 Identifying Alternatives

History teaches us that men and nations behave wisely once they have exhausted all other alternatives.

— Abba Eban (Israel Foreign Minister, quoted in The Times, London, 17 December 1970).

The issues identified in the preceding step of the case analysis provide the focus for suggesting alternative solutions. Any solution suggested must be capable of addressing at least one of the issues of concern. In general it is easier and more productive to generate solutions in groups of people although the same processes can be used by an individual with the discipline to examine issues from different perspectives and to separate the creativity of generating alternatives from the evaluation of those alternatives. This Chapter focuses on techniques for generating alternatives, preparing you for Chapter 6, where we will consider how alternatives should be evaluated. The separation of these activities in this book reflects the importance of separating these activities in the case analysis process. The process of generating alternatives is inherently creative, and nothing stifles creativity more than worrying about the feasibility or cost of alternatives. As we move forward we will rule out alternatives that fail to meet certain criteria; but sometimes an implausible alternative can be the catalyst for other creative ideas, and that is to be encouraged.

Another potential constraint on the creativity of the alternative generation process is the narrow range of experiences that we bring to bear on problems. The idea of "thinking outside the box" captures this problem. We are all boxed in by our preconceived ideas and limited life experiences. The techniques for generating alternatives discussed in this Chapter seek to force you to consider options that might not come to mind easily. The intent is to generate a rich set of alternatives to address the core issues in the case. We will examine brainstorming, de Bono's Six Hats approach, the SCAMPER technique, and variations on case-based reasoning that are developing in the artificial intelligence literature as approaches to developing alternatives.

Types of Alternatives[1]

Creating alternatives involves two separate decisions. First, you have to decide what the future will look like and, second, you have to suggest what actions would work best to address a particular issue, given a particular future state of the world. There are different techniques for generating each of these types of alternatives.

Alternatives as Hypotheses about the Future

One approach to generating alternatives is to think about the likely future facing an organization. The default approach is to assume that the future will be a continuation of the past, and most case analyses implicitly make this assumption, and so the view of alternatives as decision packages, discussed next, dominates. But another approach to generating alternatives is to systematically vary your view of the future, and then alternatives become the best approach, given the particular future state of the world you are envisioning. A common technique used to implement this approach is scenario planning.

Scenario Planning

Scenario planning begins by identifying the major factors or drivers in an organization's environment that might change and have a direct effect on the organization (see Figure 15). These may be macro-economic conditions, demographic changes, competitor behaviour or technology changes to name a few. (The "PESTLE" technique encourages you to consider political, economic, social, technological, legal and environmental factors.) Next, identify any uncertainties about these driving forces: which ones can you least predict and, therefore, will most likely catch you by surprise? The scenarios or alternative futures are then built by reasoning through the consequences of changes in these drivers. For each alternative state of the world, a specific course of action for the organization would be developed that best positions the organization within that environment. Shell Oil has been a pioneer in scenario planning and maintains a website that illustrates the approach.[2]

---

[1] This approach is based on a scientific model; see Platt. J.R. (1964). "Strong inference", *Science* 146 (3642).

[2] <http://www.shell.com/home/content/aboutshell/our_strategy/shell_global_scenarios/>

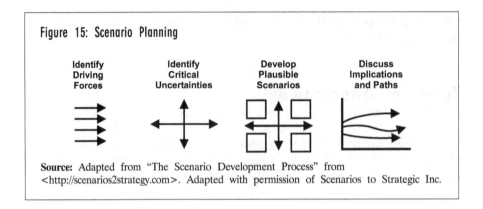

Figure 15: Scenario Planning

Identify Driving Forces

Identify Critical Uncertainties

Develop Plausible Scenarios

Discuss Implications and Paths

Source: Adapted from "The Scenario Development Process" from <http://scenarios2strategy.com>. Adapted with permission of Scenarios to Strategic Inc.

Alternatives as Decision Packages[3]

Another approach to conceptualizing your alternatives is to think of them as complex packages of decisions/actions that must be implemented as a whole to make sense. Your alternatives, therefore, are not the individual solutions to individual issues that may arise from a brainstorming session; rather they are a well-integrated set of actions that deal with all of the high priority issues. Within every state of the world there may be alternative decision packages that could be implemented. Most alternative generation techniques take a decision package approach and either implicitly or explicitly assumes a state of the world in which these decision packages can all be implemented.

Sometimes, the decision packages that case analysts identify are not true "alternatives" in the sense of being mutually exclusive courses of action. Rather each decision package is a way of dealing with some subset of issues or different, not mutually exclusive, ways of dealing with a single issue. For example, in the JetBlue case we could deal with inconvenienced passengers by apologizing, offering compensation and/or developing new policies for such situations in the future. These are not "alternatives" — all could be implemented — but there may be different costs/benefits to each decision package.

As we will see in Chapter 6: Evaluating Alternatives, there are different approaches to evaluating alternatives depending on which form they take but in the remainder of this Chapter we will focus on processes for developing alternative decision packages. There are many approaches to developing alternatives but a key distinction is whether they are "blue sky" approaches where anything is possible versus incremental approaches that start with our current position and work systematically from that position. We will examine brainstorming and de Bono's Six Hat approach as illustrations of blue sky alternative generation techniques, and the Scamper technique and risk management perspective as incremental approaches.

---

[3] This approach draws from the literature on zero based budgeting; see Lynch. T.D., (1990). *Public Budgeting in America,* 3rd Edition. Englewook Cliffs, New Jersey: Prentice Hall: pp. 51–25.

We will end with a discussion of case-based reasoning and metaphorical reasoning that encompasses both of these approaches.

Brainstorming

Brainstorming refers generally to any technique used to generate ideas or alternatives. The core idea is that the generation of alternatives should not be censored during the process. In other words the focus is on creativity, and not on feasibility, at this stage. Don't worry about the criteria that will be used to evaluate the alternatives yet, that will come up in the next stage. In brainstorming sometimes wild ideas will be put forward but rather than reacting negatively to these suggestions, they can become a catalyst for other ideas that may turn out to be useful. Let the process unfold, have fun and build on the ideas that emerge until you have a rich set of alternatives.

Brainstorming begins with the definition of the issue to be resolved. It is important that issues be defined in terms of the problem to be solved rather than in terms of a preferred alternative. For example, JetBlue appears to have an issue with its ability to handle contingencies, but stating that it needs better contingency planning as an issue presupposes the solution. It is important to frame your issues in language that encourages a wide search for solutions. Brainstorming should be used to develop alternatives for each of the high priority issues identified in the previous stage.

Brainstorming in groups can be constrained if there are differences in rank, experience etc. among group members. One variation in brainstorming procedure to deal with this is to begin with written suggestions that are then read to the group to encourage new ideas. (The "nominal group technique" uses this process and also has anonymous voting on issues to prioritize them.) Another variation is to form groups of similar people and have each group prepare a list of ideas that is then circulated to other groups, without attribution of the ideas so that the quality of the idea can be separated from the identity of the person or group who generated the idea. This is similar to the "Delphi technique", which uses a panel of experts to generate alternatives which are then anonymously fed back to the group until a consensus emerges.

In the field, brainstorming solutions to organizational issues may be enhanced by ensuring that all stakeholder groups affected by a particular set of issues encountered by an organization are represented in the process. For example, a company developing a sustainability action plan may bring in a variety of stakeholders, such as suppliers, customers, regulators, community groups, etc., to help generate alternatives for inclusion in that plan. Each stakeholder is likely to have a different perspective and background knowledge leading to a richer set of alternatives being generated. This logic can also be applied by having different members of the case analysis group role play stakeholders. It may be useful to give the group members some lead time to research their particular stakeholder's perspective.

In workshops using the JetBlue case, I have used brainstorming processes, and below is a list of alternatives that have been suggested to deal with the issues of better managing brand risk and operational risk mentioned in the previous Chapter:

- Change strategy (give up the promise never to cancel flights?)
- Slow growth to match existing operating systems to demand
- Better weather forecasting systems (or only fly in good weather markets!)
- Better on-line information systems
  o For passengers, advanced cancellations
  o For crew, contingency planning
  o For baggage, expedited recovery from cancellations
- Scenario planning exercises
  o Better anticipation (what else could shut us down?)
  o Better deployment of resources to bottlenecks
  o Better recovery plans after a problem
- Alliances with other airlines to accommodate cancelled passengers
- Cross-training of crews to allow better redeployment
- Operational efficiencies to pay for guarantees! (Management has already apologized to customers, and committed to a passenger bill of rights, and guaranteed to compensate passengers for delays regardless of the cause).

Try the techniques discussed below to see if you can add alternatives to this list.

Six Hats

Edward de Bono developed the six hats metaphor to argue that we can improve creative thinking by focusing on a problem from different perspectives (see Figure 16). He defines six distinct views and advocates using each in turn to think through issues and generate alternatives. The blue hat focuses on controlling the process and maintaining a broad overview of the problem at hand. The red hat is the emotional response to the issue. The green hat is concerned with growth and the future. The white hat ensures that we focus on data: what we have and what we need to understand the issue. The yellow hat is optimistic, suggesting the positive possibilities of every plan. The black hat, suggested to be the natural hat of most people, is to point out the downside of issues and looks for ways of minimizing risks. By looking at issues from each of these perspectives it may be possible to generate alternatives that would not have occurred to an individual or group acting on first instincts (i.e., typically with an analytic logic, black hat, perspective).

An important aspect of using the six hats technique in a group is that everyone must wear the same hat at the same time. This implies, as with the basic rule in brainstorming, that you cannot attack the perspective or censor it by bringing in other perspectives.

Figure 16: de Bono's Six Hat Thinking

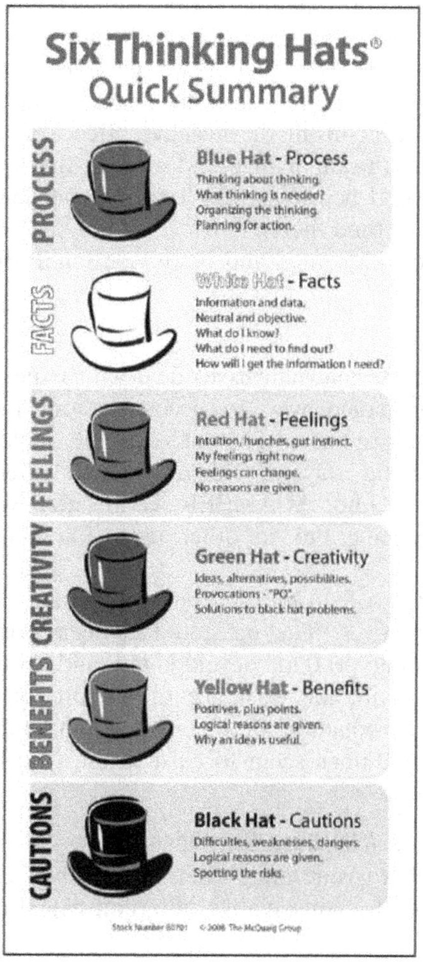

Six Thinking Hats®
Quick Summary

PROCESS

Blue Hat - Process
Thinking about thinking.
What thinking is needed?
Organizing the thinking.
Planning for action.

FACTS

White Hat - Facts
Information and data.
Neutral and objective.
What do I know?
What do I need to find out?
How will I get the information I need?

FEELINGS

Red Hat - Feelings
Intuition, hunches, gut instinct.
My feelings right now.
Feelings can change.
No reasons are given.

CREATIVITY

Green Hat - Creativity
Ideas, alternatives, possibilities.
Provocations - "PO".
Solutions to black hat problems.

BENEFITS

Yellow Hat - Benefits
Positives, plus points.
Logical reasons are given.
Why an idea is useful.

CAUTIONS

Black Hat - Cautions
Difficulties, weaknesses, dangers.
Logical reasons are given.
Spotting the risks.

Stock Number 60701   © 2006 The McQuaig Group

Source: "Six Thinking Hats: Quick Summary", by Edward de Bono, <www.debonoforschools.com>. Reprinted by permission of Lynda Curtain, *The Opportunity Thinker.*

Applying this framework to the JetBlue case, we might put on our red hat and think about how the events affect our employees' pride in their company and our customers' loyalty to the brand. We might put on the yellow hat and think about ways our response to this issue might reinforce our core values, and focus on the things that we did well during this crisis. The green hat encourages us to grow based on the experience, to think of out-of-the-box solutions — for example, perhaps we should only fly in warm weather regions (while this may sound like a trivial alternative, JetBlue did move its main hub to Florida after this event)! The white hat encourages us to go back to the data: did the markets react to the problem, or did they perceive this as a temporary issue? Why did this one location have such an effect on our entire operations (look up hub-and-spoke networks to get a sense of why)? And why were our competitors able to handle the situation better than us? The black hat draws our attention to the legal liability reputational damage, and the advantages our competitors gained. This perspective forces us to confront the negative effects of the event. The blue hat reviews our use of the other hats and ensures that each perspective has been thoroughly explored before moving on. You can learn more about the Six Thinking Hats® method here:

<www.deBonoForSchools.com> and <www.deBonoForBusiness.com>

SCAMPER Technique

One way to generate alternatives to deal with issues is to change what is currently there in some way to accommodate the identified needs or gaps in our performance. The SCAMPER technique is designed to provide a systematic way of thinking about alternatives based on changes to the status quo. SCAMPER is an acronym for "Substitute, Combine, Adapt, Magnify, Put to other uses, Eliminate and Rearrange" (see Table 3).

The weakness of the SCAMPER approach is that it is inherently conservative in its alternatives. The method has been primarily used to address issues in on-going product development and so assumes significant sunk costs associated with the existence of the product and technological commitments in the production process. This approach however may be useful where these conditions seem to exist in the case being considered.

Risk Management as Alternative Generation

Another approach to generating alternatives (that, like the SCAMPER technique, may generate conservative alternatives) draws from the risk

Table 3: SCAMPER Technique	
S	Substitute one activity or input for another
C	Combine activities or inputs
A	Adapt products or processes to new circumstances
M	Magnify or exaggerate one feature or characteristic
P	Put to other uses
E	Eliminate (or reduce) some component
R	Rearrange (reverse) the order of processes or emphases

Source: Adapted from Serrat, O. (2009). *The SCAMPER Technique*. Asian Development Bank. <http://www.adb.org/sites/default/files/pub/2009/the-scamper-technique.pdf>

management literature. Recall that in Chapter 4: Identifying Issues, we prioritized issues based on the risks they posed to the organization. The risk matrix described in that Chapter is a tool used in the risk management profession. This field also provides a typology for managing risks that may suggest alternatives to consider.

When faced with a risk, risk managers consider if there are ways to:

1. mitigate the risk
    (a) remove the risk
    (b) reduce the likelihood of occurrence
    (c) reduce the consequences
2. transfer the risk
    (a) allowing others who are better able to handle the risks to provide a service
    (b) insuring against loss so that the cost of the risk is known and manageable
3. accept the risk as an essential aspect of organizational activities.

Each of the identified high priority issues (see Figure 14: Risk Matrix) may be considered from this perspective and alternatives based on this framework can be developed.

For example, in the JetBlue case, if we focus on the weather as a risk to implementing our strategy, we might determine that we can't remove weather risk or reduce the likelihood of winter storms interrupting our services, but we may be able to reduce the consequences through better weather forecasting and contingency planning. We might also be able to transfer the risk by forming partnerships with other airlines to handle our passengers when we experience problems and by taking out weather insurance to compensate passengers for weather delays. JetBlue, for example, implemented a Customer Bill of Rights that promised compensation for delays over a certain length of time. We might also acknowledge that dealing with weather issues is a standard problem facing transportation companies and adjust our scheduling, staffing and contingency systems to handle such issues.

Case-Based Reasoning

In general, there are two main approaches to the analysis of complex problems. One form of analysis seeks to break down complex events into their constituent components and then to construct a solution based on that analysis. Most of the techniques taught in the various functional areas of business are based on this approach, and your case analysis should use these where appropriate. For example, if the case deals with a supply chain problem, there are techniques for calculating appropriate inventory levels based on the statistical characteristics of the demand and supply. Since these approaches tend to be subject matter specific; I will not deal with them in this book (but, again, I remind you that you should use these techniques where appropriate to identify issues and alternatives).

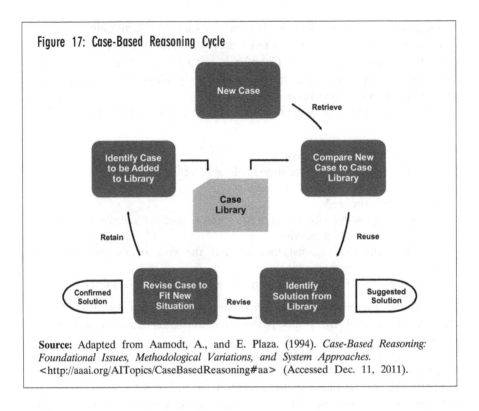

Figure 17: Case-Based Reasoning Cycle

Source: Adapted from Aamodt, A., and E. Plaza. (1994). *Case-Based Reasoning: Foundational Issues, Methodological Variations, and System Approaches.* <http://aaai.org/AITopics/CaseBasedReasoning#aa> (Accessed Dec. 11, 2011).

The other form of analysis is case-based reasoning (CBR) (see Figure 17).[4] CBR is reasoning by analogy, i.e., based on a comparison of the problem we are facing with other cases that we are familiar with, and basing our solution to the current problem on what worked in other settings.

> At the highest level of generality, a general CBR cycle may be described by the following four processes:
> (a) RETRIEVE the most similar case or cases
> (b) REUSE the information and knowledge in that case to solve the problem
> (c) REVISE the proposed solution
> (d) RETAIN the parts of this experience likely to be useful for future problem solving.

CBR involves a complex process of pattern recognition by which an experienced analyst can process data on a large number of factors and identify a class of problems to which the present situation belongs, and/or to identify a class of solutions that have been shown to work in these situations. If you have been exposed to a large number of cases in the course of your degree program and supplemental reading, it is likely that you have a repertoire of patterns in your memory. The "trick" is to use that pattern recognition capability as a starting point for alternative gener-

---

[4] See Kolodner. J.L. (1992). "An Introduction to Case-Based Reasoning", *Artificial Intelligence Review.* V6: 3-34.

ation. Remember that even though you recognize the pattern, this does not mean that what worked elsewhere will work exactly the same in the present case. These patterns, however, can provide a starting point for further brainstorming (the "revise" portion of this technique).

If you compare the process of case-based reasoning to Kolb's learning cycle (Figure 3), you will notice similarities. Your mental library of cases is built from the concrete experiences you have had; on reflection, you have drawn lessons from these cases about how the world works; you have abstracted these lessons into general patterns that you can now recognize in new situations; and, you can experiment with these patterns to generate new alternatives that you can apply in novel situations. Case-based reasoning reflects the pattern of learning identified by Kolb.

The artificial intelligence literature on CBR suggests that while people are good at recognizing patterns, they are not as good at maintaining a comprehensive library of possibilities. The work in this field is seeking to develop decision-aides that will allow decision-makers to search for cases with the key characteristics of the current problem. This is another situation where working in groups and using the "wisdom of crowds" may help you to find appropriate cases to help develop solutions. The joint experience of everyone in the group will provide a richer set of possible analogies than will be possessed by any individual.

If we apply case-based reasoning to the JetBlue case, we need to identify the key characteristics of this case and search for analogous cases that might provide guidance. For example, we might look for cases dealing with small airlines and how they developed over time, or cases where companies dealt with significant public relations issues. You should think through what other features of this situation could be used to identify analogous experiences. This is an important judgment skill, and will be improved with practice. The various frameworks and theories that you have been exposed to in your education will also serve as templates for identifying key features of cases.

Benchmarking

The case-based reasoning approach to identifying alternatives is conceptually related to the concept of benchmarking, which involves the search for alternatives by comparing our circumstances to those of others. So, for example, we might examine best practices in the industry for dealing with any of the issues that we have identified in the JetBlue case or identify analogous processes to which we might benchmark JetBlue's performance (see Table 4). Benchmarking looks for examples of how to handle issues either within the current organization or in the behaviour of external organizations. Benchmarking can also look at best-practices for a specific function or process, or seek analogies to the present issue (e.g., perhaps handling a weather problem at an airline is analogous to handling a product recall at a food or drug company).

Table 4: Types of Benchmarking

Type of Benchmarking	Variation	Description
Internal	Historic	How have we handled issues in the past?
	Unit	How have different units in the business handled this issue?
External	Functional	How have other industries handled this issue?
	Analogous	How have other companies handled analogous issues?

Metaphorical Reasoning

Case-based reasoning operates by analogy. As this has developed in the artificial intelligence literature the analogies are fairly literal. We can use similar organizations or situations to identify risks, alternatives, etc. But it may also be useful for generating alternatives to frame the issues metaphorically. A metaphor is a way of describing or seeing one thing in terms of the characteristics of another. For example, business practice can be described as a game, a war, survival of the fittest, a cosy club, etc.[5] Gareth Morgan has inventoried the main metaphors for thinking about or-

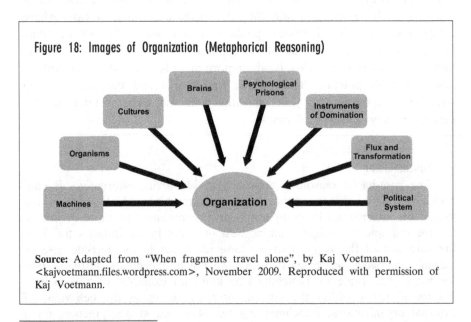

Figure 18: Images of Organization (Metaphorical Reasoning)

Source: Adapted from "When fragments travel alone", by Kaj Voetmann, <kajvoetmann.files.wordpress.com>, November 2009. Reproduced with permission of Kaj Voetmann.

---

[5] On this technique, I am guided by Schön, D. (1978). "Generative Metaphor: A Perspective on Problem Setting in Social Policy." In A. Ortony (1986/1997) (Ed.). *Metaphor and Thought.* Cambridge: Cambridge University Press and Morgan, Gareth, *Images of Organisation*, Sage.

ganizations seen in the literature and these are summarized in Figure 18. Each of these metaphors brings out different aspects of what a business is and does.

By reframing issues according to different metaphors, it is possible to generate unique alternatives. The approach to alternative generation that this logic suggests is to search for metaphors that capture key aspects of the issue. For example, should we regard the JetBlue incident of passengers being held for 11 hours in a plane on the runway as optimism, kidnapping, incompetence, promise keeping, etc.? How we frame this incident will have different implications for what we should do about it in the future.

Chapter Summary

Once the issues have been identified and prioritized, your creativity and knowledge can be used to generate alternatives that have the potential to address the key problems or opportunities facing the organization. The process of generating alternatives must be separated from the process of evaluating alternatives in order to create a rich set of possibilities. This is a creative process that can be based on the innate creativity of individuals (brainstorming), or by systematically looking at the problem from multiple perspectives (six hats method), considering how to move incrementally from where we are to deal with an issue (SCAMPER method, risk management techniques), or by using analogies and metaphors to help identify alternatives (case based reasoning). The key to generating a rich set of alternatives is not to censor the process; do not worry about whether or not an alternative can be implemented, just keep throwing out ideas until you or the group cannot think of anything new. The next stage in the process will evaluate your alternatives, and identify the one that best addresses the issues identified.

Problems

1. What factors should you consider when using scenario planning?

2. Summarize the Brainstorming approach to identifying alternatives.

3. List and compare the six hats approaches to alternative generation.

4. Identify typical approaches to risk used by risk managers. How do these help generate alternatives?

5. Differentiate the main types of benchmarking.

Exercises

1. You have invited friends over for dinner but you were distracted, and the meal was burned. People are expected to arrive within 30 minutes. Identify some (at least 10) alternatives for dealing with this situation. Be creative and don't censor yourself!

2. There is considerable evidence that human activity is approaching the limits of sustainability of the ecosystem. Generate alternatives for dealing with this problem. Try this exercise by yourself, then recruit three or four others to join in the exercise. Finally, try an internet search of the topic and look for the most outrageous suggestions. Compare the results and identify why they differed.

3. Refer to Appendix C: Eisner's Mousetrap (Disney). Use the core issues that you identified previously (Chapter 4: Identifying Issues, Exercises) and develop alternatives that could address these issues. Use at least two of the methods discussed in this Chapter.

6 Evaluating Alternatives

At this point in the case analysis process you should have a rich range ofhttp://www.facebook.com/ alternatives to consider. In order to reduce this set to the one alternative that you would recommend (or implement if you are the decision-maker), you need to evaluate each alternative based on a set of criteria that reflects the objectives of the decision-maker. If there is a single objective, then the evaluation process is relatively simple. The alternatives can be ranked according to the decision criteria and the alternative that maximizes the objective is selected. If the data and the decision-maker's objective are quantitative then standard evaluative procedures can be used (e.g., net present value, expected value, etc.). Even in these cases, however, it is standard procedure to consider qualitative factors before committing to the results of a quantitative analysis. In most case analyses (and real life), however, decision-making criteria are not this simple. It is more common that decision-makers face multiple objectives (for example, cost, quality and time are frequently used criteria for new product development) and achieving one is often accomplished at the expense of another. This situation requires specific techniques for evaluating alternatives on multiple criteria.

Recall in the previous Chapter that different forms of "alternatives", or potential solutions, were described. This Chapter starts by mapping the logic of evaluating alternatives into the different forms of alternatives. The main focus of the Chapter, however, is on techniques for evaluating alternatives as decision packages when there are multiple objectives or multiple attributes of alternatives that must be taken into account.

The Logic of Evaluating Alternatives

Before we examine specific techniques for evaluating alternatives, we need to step back and look at the logic of this process. Too often case analysts present "alternatives" that aren't really alternatives — i.e., mutually exclusive courses of action — and so the recommendation is to implement all of the "alternatives" (a logical impossibility)! There are a number of ways of conceptualizing alternatives that may help focus your work before you begin the evaluation process.

Let's begin with a basic model. There are two dimensions to the problem of recommending a course of action in case analysis. First, we have to identify the likely future conditions in which the decision-maker will be operating. This is often referred to as a future "state of the world." Second, in each possible state of the world, we need to identify the best course of action for the decision-maker. Our analysis of alternatives proceeds sequentially through these two dimensions: first, make your prediction about the state of the world that will exist; second, make your recommendation about the best course of action in this state of the world. These two dimensions require different forms of evaluation.

It is important to spend some time formulating your alternatives before you move into the evaluation phase, and understanding whether they are alternatives for different states of the world versus decision packages for a particular state of the world (refer to Types of Alternatives in Chapter 5: Identifying Alternatives). For example, in the JetBlue case, one state of the world would be where the storm is a one-in-a-million event that would probably never reoccur, while another state of the world would be where weather disruptions are regarded as a recurring issue. Depending on which state of the world exists, you would probably recommend very different decision packages for management to consider. These two types of alternatives must be clearly separated as the form of evaluation will differ.[1]

For example, if our alternatives reflect different assumptions about the world, and each alternative can satisfy the objectives of the decision-maker given the state of the world, then we can test the alternative states of the world against our data to determine which is most likely to be true. The matrix in Table 5 reflects a method used in the military intelligence community to evaluate the likelihood of future events known as "Analysis of Competing Hypotheses" (ACH).[2] The alternative states of the world, or hypotheses, are arrayed across the top, and our key pieces of evidence (e.g., market projections, knowledge of competition behaviour, etc.) are listed down the side. A judgment is then made whether a particular piece of evidence is consistent (+) or inconsistent (–) with that alternative being true. Only evidence that is "diagnostic," i.e., that is material and varies between alternatives, is considered. The analysis may also consider the quality of the evidence in reaching a final conclusion. The final judgment is based on the balance of probabilities that the evidence supports a par-

---

[1] One technique that combines both approaches is decision tree analysis. This approach works for simple choices, but is not easily applicable to strategic questions.

[2] See Heuer Jr., R.J. (1999). *Psychology of Intelligence Analysis*. Center for the Study of Intelligence. (At <http://www.cia.gov/csi/books/19104/index.html>)

Table 5: Analysis of Competing Hypotheses

	Evidence Quality	Alternative 1	Alternative 2	Alternative 3
Evidence 1	High		–	+
Evidence 2	High	–	–	+
Evidence 3	Low		–	+
Evidence 4	Medium	–	+	–

ticular alternative being true.[3] For example, in Table 5 we would conclude that, on balance, the evidence supports Alternative 3 being true.

It is important to note that because this approach is rooted in the scientific literature, the evidence can never prove that an alternative is true, but it can be used to reject false hypotheses. At the end of the analysis the best that we can say is that a certain alternative is most likely to be true given a particular set of evidence. New evidence may change our conclusion.

Where our alternatives represent different decision packages appropriate for a given state of the world, a more elaborate decision process is used. Two situations are possible. First, if the decision-packages being considered are not truly alternatives but rather a set of actions that could each be implemented, then one approach to evaluating them would be to rank order the decision-packages according to their cost/benefit ratio. Assuming there is a budget constraint, all alternatives with a cost/benefit ratio < 1 (i.e., the benefits exceed the costs) would be implemented until we reach our budget constraint.

Second, if the decision-packages are mutually exclusive, then we need to compare each decision package based on how well they meet the decision-maker's objectives. The techniques described below assume that you have made a decision about the state of the world and you are evaluating alternative ways of acting given that state of the world. It is important that you do not try to evaluate alternatives that span both states of the world and decision-packages within a particular state of the world. (For example, this would be like trying to evaluate the following alternatives: (1) should I wear a raincoat when it rains or (2) should I wear sunglasses when it is sunny. You will probably end up recommending both "alternatives" and miss the real question of what the weather is going to be like.)

---

[3] This method can be further developed based on Bayesian statistics. See Valtorta, M., Dang, J., Goradia, H., Huang, J., and Huhns, M. (2011) "Extending Heuer's Analysis of Competing Hypotheses Method" <http://www.cse.sc.edu/~mgv/reports/IA-05.pdf> to Support Complex Decision Analysis.

Screening Alternatives

A starting point for the evaluation process described below is to screen the alternatives to eliminate any alternatives that are not worth detailed analysis. The alternatives that pass these screens are then subject to closer scrutiny and more formal evaluation. In constructing our alternatives we know that they all address at least one of the issues that we have identified, and that they contribute towards meeting the decision-maker's objectives; but now we need to compare our alternatives to each other to determine which one we should recommend for implementation.

Feasibility

The process for generating alternatives has focused on creativity and productivity (i.e., generating many imaginative alternatives). This means that some alternatives may not be feasible. Recall that one of the goals of reading the case is to identify constraints facing the decision-maker. This is the time to bring those constraints into the process to eliminate alternatives that fail the feasibility test. Key constraints may include:

- Legal and ethical proscriptions on actions
- Resource constraints (at this point in the analysis they must be absolute constraints: i.e., it is not a question of the relative cost of an alternative compared with other alternatives, but of its absolute cost compared with the company's resources)
- Technological constraints (i.e., the technology to implement the alternative is not available)
- Strategic constraints (any strategic commitment that supersedes the immediate issue should be considered a constraint in the short run)
- Implementation constraints (a key constraint is time, a solution that requires too much time to implement might not address the issue before the organization fails or an opportunity passes by).

Dominance

Another approach to screening alternatives is to eliminate any alternatives that are dominated by others. An alternative, "A," is dominated if there is another alternative, "B," that does everything that alternative A does and at least one thing better. For example, assuming that minimizing cost is always an objective, then the only alternative that needs to be brought forward is the lowest cost alternative among those that accomplish the same ends. In order to implement screening based on dominance, however, we need to know the decision-maker's objectives in detail (this task is described below). Note that where alternatives differ on multiple criteria it may not be possible to eliminate any alternatives based on the dominance criteria — instead we need to examine the trade-offs among different objectives within each alternative.

The alternatives that survive the screening process described above are viable candidates for addressing the issues identified. Recall that another task in reading the case is to identify the objectives of the decision-maker. It is likely that each alternative will have different capabilities and costs compared with the objectives of the decision-maker. Our final evaluation determines how well these alternatives meet the decision-maker's objectives.

Identifying Objectives

Unfortunately most of the decision-making models that are taught in professional schools assume the decision-maker's objective(s) and so students frequently also assume the objectives of decision-makers and other stakeholders in cases rather than formally analyzing these objectives. One of my favourite cases concerns Patagonia, a maker of high-end outdoor equipment.[4] Patagonia is a closely held company whose owners are outdoors enthusiasts and innovators. Their objectives for the company are to make enough profit to be able to provide stable employment for their employees, support environmental causes and maintain the owners' lifestyle. They are not interested in maximizing profit or market share, or any of the usual business objectives. In fact, they regard high growth rates as a "problem." Students examining the Patagonia case are frequently confused by the objectives of the company, and even suggest that a change of ownership is necessary to allow the business to pursue the "right" objectives! There are no "right" objectives in practice, there are only objectives and whatever those objectives are must drive the analysis.

In practice, the process of identifying objectives is complex. For example, a decision-maker may face different objectives than other stakeholders in the case, and we must decide how to reconcile those personal objectives with the objectives embedded in a particular role; or a decision-maker may face conflicting objectives (e.g., growth versus short-run profitability). It is important in case analysis to correctly identify the objectives of the decision-maker prior to evaluating the alternatives.

Objectives, Attributes, Criteria

The first step is to identify what is valued or preferred by the decision-maker. The second step is to identify the attributes of alternatives that would contribute to achieving what is valued. For example, if a decision-maker values wealth creation, this must still be translated into the attributes of alternatives that will lead to wealth creation, such as customer satisfaction, cost control, innovation, etc. The criteria used to evaluate alternatives are operational versions of the attributes of alternatives that will contribute to achieving the values of decision-makers.

---

[4] Merchant, K. (2007). "Patagonia, Inc.", *Management Control Systems, Second Edition.* Edinburgh Gate: UK. Prentice Hall.

Three types of criteria are possible:[5] natural, proxy and constructed. Natural criteria are measures that are obviously and directly related to the attribute, such as using measures of market share to judge how well an alternative meets the attribute of increasing market share. Proxy criteria are not direct measures, but reflect a causal connection to the attribute of interest. For example, if we cannot measure market share directly perhaps we use brand recognition as a proxy criterion. Constructed criteria like proxy criteria are not directly related to the attribute of interest and reflect a theoretical linkage, for example: if we have a model of demand for our product we might monitor changes in the input variables, such as demographics, income levels, etc., within a market that we plan to enter to construct a criterion to suggest how our market share will be affected.

In most case analyses where the evaluation is occurring ex post (i.e., we cannot go back in time and collect the data we would really like) only natural and proxy criteria are available. Where a proxy criterion is used, the logic connecting this to the attributes of interest must be made explicit. In most cases natural criteria will be used, and the distinction between attributes and criteria is not crucial.

Causal Mapping

One approach to identifying the linkages between actions and the achievement of values is causal mapping. A causal map is simply a graphic device that uses lines to link actions and outcomes. Each line represents a causal connection. This approach has been adopted by Kaplan and Norton in the concept of strategy mapping (see Figure 19) that has been used to develop and implement the Balanced Scorecard.[6] Although their approach imposes constraints on the structure of the map and what may be included, the logic underlying their approach is consistent with causal mapping.

Based on the strategy map in Figure 19, we might suggest that the objective of the decision-maker is to improve overall returns and any alternatives might contribute to this objective if they broaden revenue mix or improve operating efficiency (for example based on the strategy map provided). These attributes of alternatives could be converted into specific criteria, such as operationalizing revenue mix as the percentage of revenue from our three top selling products, or operationalizing operating efficiency as the selling, general and administrative cost per dollar of revenue.

Once the objectives have been clarified, then we are in a position to do a detailed evaluation of alternatives. Remember to use the dominance criteria described above for additional screening of alternatives now that the detailed objectives have been identified.

---

[5] Keeney, R.L. (1992). *Value Focused Thinking: A Path to Creative Decision Making.* Cambridge, Mass.: Harvard University Press,

[6] Kaplan, R.S., Norton, D.P. (2004). *Stratgey Maps: Converting Intangible Assets into Tangible Outcomes.* Boston: Harvard Business School Press.

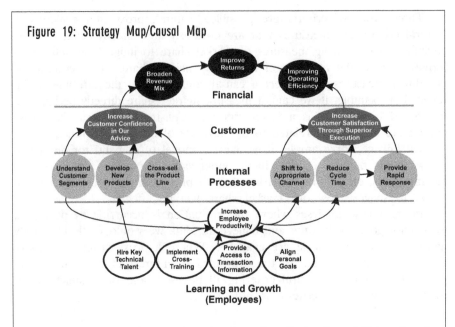

Figure 19: Strategy Map/Causal Map

Improve
Returns

Broaden
Revenue
Mix

Improving
Operating
Efficiency

Financial

Increase
Customer Confidence
in Our
Advice

Customer

Increase
Customer Satisfaction
Through Superior
Execution

Understand
Customer
Segments

Develop
New
Products

Cross-sell
the Product
Line

**Internal
Processes**

Shift to
Appropriate
Channel

Reduce
Cycle
Time

Provide
Rapid
Response

Increase
Employee
Productivity

Hire Key
Technical
Talent

Implement
Cross-
Training

Provide
Access to
Transaction
Information

Align
Personal
Goals

**Learning and Growth
(Employees)**

Source: Strategic Mapping, "A Balancing Act — Part 2", by Howard Rohm, Dec 6, 2011, <www.enterpriseleadership.org>. Reproduced with permission of Balanced Scorecard Institute.

Multi-attribute Decision-making

It is most likely that multiple objectives and/or multiple attributes will be identified in the case. The evaluation process has to capture the relative importance of these attributes in order to identified preferred alternatives among a set where each alternative has pros and cons.

Force Field Analysis

The simplest method of analysis of alternatives is to list the pros and cons of each alternative and then to make a holistic judgement about the relative value of each alternative. A visual tool, force field analysis, for this approach comes from the change management literature.[7] The idea behind force field analysis is that every alternative course of action has forces pushing for its implementation and counterforces pushing to block it (or maintain the status quo). The likelihood of an alternative being implemented depends on the balance of these positive and negative forces. Force field analysis takes this simple idea and creates a visual representation of it as shown in Figure 20.

Force field analysis can be used as a holistic evaluation tool or converted into a quantitative method. When it is used holistically, after the

---

[7] This approach is derived from Lewin, K. (1951). *Field theory in social science*. London: Harper Row.

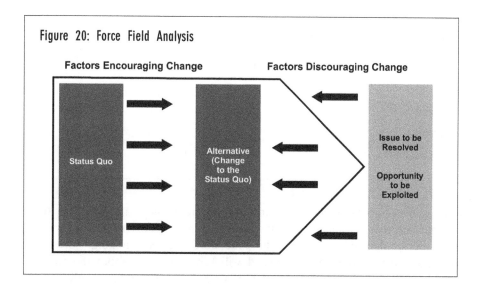

Figure 20: Force Field Analysis

Factors Encouraging Change   **Factors Discouraging Change**

Status Quo

Alternative (Change to the Status Quo)

Issue to be Resolved

Opportunity to be Exploited

forces for and against an alternative have been identified, the case analyst (or group) must decide, on balance, whether an alternative could be successfully implemented. A further judgment is made, across all alternatives, as to which alternative is most favoured for implementation by the forces affecting the overall change. The method can be quantified by having the case analyst (or group) assign scale values (e.g., on a 1 to 5 scale) representing the strength of a particular force (i.e., each arrow in Figure 20 would be assigned a value). For each alternative, the sum of negative forces is subtracted from the sum of positive forces to calculate the net force on the alternative. Only those alternatives with net positive forces would be compared further, and the alternative with the largest positive score value would be the most likely alternative to be implemented successfully.

Force field analysis may be a useful adjunct to the other evaluation techniques discussed below in that it forces the analysis to consider the full range of factors that may affect the likely success of the alternative.

Decision Matrix

A common approach to multi-attribute decision-making in case analysis is to construct a decision matrix listing the alternatives across one axis and the criteria to be used to evaluate the alternatives across the other axis as shown in Table 6. Each alternative is judged on its ability to meet each criterion on a subjective scale. (Typically a five-point scale is used, where a higher number indicates that the Alternative better meets that criterion. Arbitrary numbers have been used in this table to illustrate the technique.) This method assumes that it is possible to rank order alternatives on each of the criteria.

Note that the "overall score" shown in Table 6 has no real meaning. Since our judgment is comparative, as long as the numbers show us our

Table 6: Decision Matrix Template

	Alternative 1	Alternative 2	Alternative 3
Criterion 1	2	2	5
Criterion 2	5	4	4
Criterion 3	5	5	2
Overall Score	12	11	11

ranking of alternatives (i.e., a relative preference), the scale on which they are measured is irrelevant. In the example shown, Alternative 1 appears to be the preferred alternative. But take note that our ranking scores are close together. In the next Chapter I will raise concerns about the robustness of our recommendations and the need to do sensitivity analysis and other validation procedures.

The approach described above makes the simplifying assumption that all criteria are equal in deciding the preferred alternative. A variation on this approach is to determine the relative weight of different criteria, and to use the weighted average score in determining the ranking of alternatives (see Table 7). The weights across all criteria sum to 1, and represent the relative importance of each criterion to the decision-maker. (This is a convention, but the same results would be obtained by using whole numbers to represent the relative importance of the criteria.) For example, is it more important to achieve high quality or low cost, is it better to have higher customer satisfaction or higher return on investment? The example uses the same ratings as the previous table, but now weighted based on a subjective evaluation of the importance of the criteria. Note that Alternative 3 now appears to be the preferred alternative.

One approach to creating weights is by pairwise comparison of the criteria. For each possible pair of criteria, decide which criterion is preferred. The weight attached to any criterion will be the number of times

Table 7: Decision Matrix with Weighted Criteria

Criterion	Weight	Alternative 1 — Unweighted Rating	Weighted Rating	Alternative 2 — Unweighted Rating	Weighted Rating	Alternative 3 — Unweighted Rating	Weighted Rating
#1	0.5	2	1.0	2	1.0	5	2.5
#2	0.3	5	1.5	4	1.2	4	0.8
#3	0.2	5	1.0	5	1.0	2	0.4
Overall Score			3.5		3.2		3.9

that a criterion is preferred divided by the total number of comparisons made. In the tables above there are three criteria, so there would be three pairwise comparisons (1 vs. 2, 1 vs. 3, 2 vs. 3). One problem with this approach is that the lowest weighted criterion will always be zero. An arbitrary low weight is usually given to keep this criterion in the evaluation process. The need to provide a better method for identifying the relative importance of multiple attributes has motivated work on multi-attribute decision theory. One approach to this, the analytic hierarchy process, is discussed below.

Analytic Hierarchy Process[8]

The analytic hierarchy process provides a mathematical way of comparing alternatives across multiple attributes. The technique requires a series of pairwise comparisons that may be easier to handle than comparing a large number of alternatives simultaneously. The "hierarchy" referred to in this technique is the relationship between the objective, criteria and alternatives diagrammed in Figure 21. The approach can be summarized in the seven steps shown below.

To illustrate this technique I will assume that I am purchasing a car. I am considering three alternatives, and my criteria are price, style and efficiency of the cars. I will refer to my three alternatives simply as A, B and C so as not to offend any car makers or fans of particular brands. The three alternatives all address my basic issue of finding reliable transportation within my limited budget (i.e., they are all feasible but none dominate).

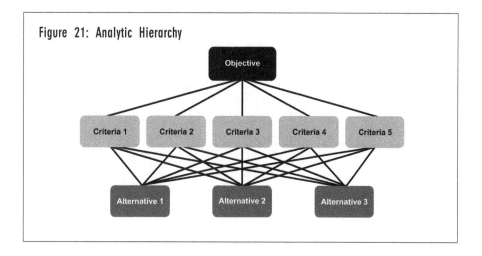

Figure 21: Analytic Hierarchy

---

[8] An excellent tutorial on the use of the AHP is available at Teknomo, K. (2006) *Analytic Hierarchy Process (AHP) Tutorial*: <http://people.revoledu.com/kardi/tutorial/AHP/>. Another useful tutorial is <http://www.booksites.net/download/coyle/student_files/AHP_Technique.pdf>. An online calculator for priorities and consistency measures is available at <http://www.isc.senshu-u.ac.jp/~thc0456/EAHP/AHPweb.html>.

Step 1: Create Matrices

The first step is to create square matrices for the alternatives and criteria. There will be one matrix for the criteria that lists all the criteria on each axis. This matrix will be used to determine how trade-offs between criteria will be handled. At the moment the matrix is blank except for "1" along the diagonal (since anything compared with itself will be regarded as equal).

Criteria Comparison Matrix

	Price	**Style**	**Efficiency**
Price	1		
Style		1	
Efficiency			1

There will also be separate matrices for each criterion with the alternatives listed on each axis. These matrices will be used to determine how the alternatives compare against each criterion considered independently (later steps will combine these comparisons).

Price Comparison Matrix

	A	**B**	**C**
A	1		
B		1	
C			1

Style Comparison Matrix

	A	**B**	**C**
A	1		
B		1	
C			1

Efficiency Comparison Matrix

	A	**B**	**C**
A	1		
B		1	
C			1

Step 2: Pairwise Comparisons of Alternatives

For each criterion, compare each alternative to each of the others (i.e., a series of pairwise comparisons). For each pair of alternatives, rate which alternative best meets the criteria on a scale ranging from 1 (there is no difference between alternatives) to 9 (one alternative clearly dominates the other on this criteria) (see Table 8). In the matrix, enter the value for the comparison and the inverse of the value for the other comparison. For example, if alternative A is rated as clearly better than alternative B on the criteria, then enter 9 in cell AB and 1/9 in cell BA.

Repeat the above procedure for each criterion. You will now have matrices showing how each alternative compares on your criteria considered independently, but the problem is to make a decision based on all of the criteria. This is addressed in the next step.

For the car purchase example, I begin by comparing each pair of alternatives based on their "price." This is the simple criterion to compare. I can order the prices of the cars and note that A<B<C, with C being very expensive compared with A, and B being slightly more expensive. I also have to take into account the lifetime cost of ownership, and estimate the costs of routine maintenance and the cost of repairs. These comparisons are reflected in the matrix below.

Table 8: Analytic Hierarchy Scale Values

Scale Description (Alternative A compared to Alternative B)	Value	Inverse (B to A)
A is clearly preferred to B on this criterion	9	1/9 (0.111)
	8	1/8 (0.125)
A is very strongly preferred to B on this criterion	7	1/7 (0.143)
	6	1/6 (0.167)
A is strongly preferred to B on this criterion	5	1/5 (0.200)
	4	1/4 (0.250)
A is moderately preferred to B on this criterion	3	1/3 (0.333)
	2	1/2 (0.500)
A and B appear equal on this criterion	1	1

Price Comparison Matrix

	A	B	C
A	1.000	3.000	9.000
B	0.333	1.000	2.000
C	0.111	0.500	1.000
SUM	1.444	4.500	12.000

All of the cars are relatively close in their styling, since they are all compact sedans, but I prefer A to B and C, and I prefer the styling of B to C. Style in this case may be a combination of aesthetics and the features that each car offers. These judgements are reflected in the matrix below.

Style Comparison Matrix

	A	B	C
A	1.000	2.000	3.000
B	0.500	1.000	1.000
C	0.333	1.000	1.000
SUM	1.833	4.000	5.000

Finally I compare each pair of cars on their fuel efficiency. In this case B is the most fuel efficient, followed by C, with A being least efficient. These comparisons also have to take into account my likely driving habits, so that the published average fuel economy can be adjusted to the mix of city and highway driving I anticipate doing and the total distance I will travel. These comparisons are reflected in the matrix below.

Efficiency Comparison Matrix

	A	B	C
A	1.000	0.333	0.500
B	3.000	1.000	3.000
C	2.000	0.333	1.000
SUM	6.000	1.667	4.500

Step 3: Pairwise Comparisons of Criteria

The same comparison procedure is applied to the criterion against which the alternatives are to be compared. The question being posed this time is how willing the decision-maker would be to sacrifice one criterion to achieve another. This decision is again made on a nine-point scale, and the ratings (and the inverses) are entered into the criterion comparison matrix.

In the example, price and efficiency are equally important to me, but I am more willing to trade-off style for price than I am for efficiency. This is a crucial matrix that will differentiate people's choices. For example, if someone valued style more than efficiency, it is likely the final results will change.

Criteria Comparison Matrix

	Price	Style	Efficiency
Price	1.000	7.000	1.000
Style	0.143	1.000	0.250
Efficiency	1.000	4.000	1.000
Sum	2.143	12.000	2.250

Step 4: Calculate Priority Scores for Alternatives

Each of the matrices described above (one for each criterion comparing alternatives, and one for the comparison across criteria) are now used to calculate the priority given to each alternative on each criterion. This is done by calculating the sum of all ratings across a row divided by the total ratings in the matrix. (Technically this calculates the principal right eigenvalue: there are easily available software programs and Excel add-ons to do these calculations.[9]) This procedure will give a priority to each alternative on each criterion where the sum of priorities across the alternatives equals 1.

The output from an AHP spreadsheet for my alternatives across all of the criteria is shown below.

Alternative	Price	Style	Efficiency
A	0.703	0.548	0.626
B	0.207	0.241	0.224
C	0.090	0.211	0.151

Step 5: Calculate Priority Scores for Criteria

The procedures described in Step 4 are also applied to the matrix of ratings of criteria to calculate the priority of each criterion in achieving the overall objective. Again, the procedure will provide priorities that sum to 1 across all criteria.

As you should be able to anticipate given the discussion above, in the example, the most important criterion is price, with efficiency coming in a

---

[9] See, for example, Teknomo, K. (2006) *Analytic Hierarchy Process (AHP) Tutorial.* <http://people.revoledu.com/kardi/tutorial/AHP/> (Accessed Jan. 2012)

close second, and style being a relatively low weighted criterion in my decision.

Criterion	Criterion Weighting
Price	0.498
Style	0.087
Efficiency	0.415

Step 6: Calculate Preference Scores for Alternatives

The final rating of each alternative is the sum of the priority weighting of that alternative on each criterion multiplied by the priority weighting of each criterion. This allows each alternative to be compared across all criteria to all other alternatives. The alternative that achieves the highest score is the preferred alternative.

The results for the car purchase example are shown below. Overall, alternative A appears to be the best choice for me, given my criteria and my willingness to make trade-offs among these criteria.

Alternative	Priority Ranking of Alternatives
A	0.464
B	0.368
C	0.168

Step 7: Calculate Consistency Scores and Conclude Analysis

The final decision about alternatives must be left to the decision-maker, and further techniques of testing the reasonableness of the recommendation are provided in the next Chapter; but within this technique it is also important to ensure that the judgments that constructed the matrices are consistent (i.e., if A is preferred to B, and B is preferred to C, then A should be preferred to C). Software that implements the Analytic Hierarchy Process will calculate a consistency index for each matrix. These should all show less than 10% inconsistency before any reliance is placed on the results.

For the car purchase example, my pairwise comparisons across all of the matrices above appear to be reasonably consistent, so I can rely on the results.

Consistency of Comparisons	
Price Comparison Matrix	0.016
Style Comparison Matrix	0.016
Efficiency Comparison Matrix	0.046
Criterion Comparison Matrix	0.030

There is a significant literature evaluating the analytic hierarchy process technique and it should not be used in practice without consulting this literature, but it provides an example of how multiple attributes can be incorporated into the evaluation of alternatives.

The field of multi-attribute decision making is well developed and there are many other techniques that can be, and have been, applied to decision problems. Given the focus of this text on those techniques that are simple to apply and provide gains in the quality of decision-making, I will not review any of these techniques, but if you are engaged in a decision-making problem with significant consequences and deeply held views of the values to be considered, then you may wish to consider these techniques.

Chapter Summary

The alternative generation process should yield a rich set of possibilities for dealing with the issues in your case. This set of alternatives must be narrowed down to a recommendation. It is important to understand the type of alternatives that are being evaluated to choose the right method of analysis. A key distinction is whether alternatives represent different bets on the future versus different decision-packages for the decision-maker to implement. Most techniques focus on the latter type of alternatives. In part, alternatives may be eliminated if they are not feasible, i.e., they come up against a hard constraint, such as the time available, technology limits or (absolute) cost limits. Alternatives may also be eliminated if they are dominated by other alternatives; i.e., a dominant alternative is one that does everything another alternative does and at least one thing better. The key method of eliminating alternatives is to compare each alternative against the objectives of the decision-maker. This requires that the decision-maker's objectives be translated into attributes of the alternatives (e.g., making profit gets translated into gaining market share and raising margins) and specific criteria that can be compared across alternatives. Cause mapping can help to translate objectives into attributes and criteria. In most cases, decision-makers have multiple objectives (or multiple attributes that could lead to one objective), and it is necessary to examine trade-offs between these objectives (attributes). The most common approach to this problem is to use a decision matrix or weighted decision matrix, but more sophisticated multi-attribute decision methods such as the analytic hierarchy process, are also available. The overall process described in this Chapter is summarized in Figure 22.[10]

---

[10] This presentation follows the example provided by Decisions Based on Analysis of Alternatives (AoA), Dr. David G. Ullman, January 2009, available at:
<http://www.robustdecisions.com/AOA.pdf>.

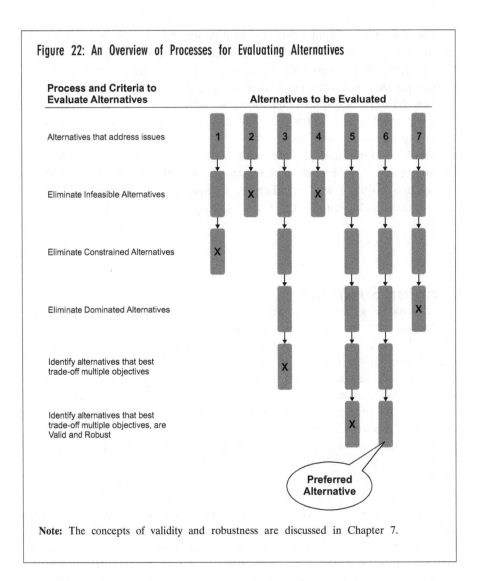

Figure 22: An Overview of Processes for Evaluating Alternatives

Note: The concepts of validity and robustness are discussed in Chapter 7.

Problems

1. Identify the two classes of alternatives. How do these types of alternatives differ?

2. Summarize the key constraints that need to be considered when screening alternatives in order to determine feasibility.

3. List and describe three types of criteria used when evaluating alternatives against our objectives.

4. Provide an overview of the processes and criteria used to evaluate alternatives.

Exercises

1. Consider your last major purchase (e.g., computer, car, house, degree program) and identify your objective(s) in making that purchase, the attributes of the alternatives that were important to you, and how you measured (including subjective judgement) each attribute. Construct a decision matrix of your decision, and evaluate the result.

2. Using the same attributes developed in the exercise above, construct an analytic hierarchy process, and compare your results to the decision matrix results.

3. The case analysis process involves complex qualitative judgments. Many of the techniques in this Chapter are designed to provide structure to these judgments, but they do not replace sound judgment. For each technique in this Chapter, identify the judgments that are required and the type of data that would support each judgment.

7 Making Recommendations

> Be willing to make decisions. That's the most important quality in a good leader. Don't fall victim to what I call the 'ready-aim-aim-aim-aim syndrome'. You must be willing to fire.
>
> T. Boone Pickens
> www.boonepickens.com

The end point of a case analysis is a recommendation for action and, depending on the requirements of the case and circumstances, an implementation plan.[1] The evaluation of alternatives should provide you with good reasons for your recommendation, but it is always a good idea to "look before you leap". In case analysis this means doing a final check to ensure that nothing has been missed in your analysis, and that the preferred alternative will be acceptable to stakeholders. This can be seen as auditing your analysis before going public with the document. This is the key stage to ensure that various biases (see Appendix A: Decision-Making Biases, and Table 2) have not entered into your case analysis process.

This Chapter begins by reviewing some audit procedures that you can use to ensure that your case analysis is thorough, and to reduce the likelihood that bias has crept into your procedures. Once you have established the validity of your recommendation, the Chapter then reviews alternative formats for reporting your case analysis.

Blind Spot Analysis[2]

Blind spot analysis is an audit procedure to ensure that you have undertaken a thorough case analysis. This involves re-examining your procedures

---

[1] <http://www.boonepickens.com/thoughts/default.asp>

[2] For further discussion of this approach see Fleisher, C., and Bensoussan, B., (2002). *Strategic and Competitive Analysis: Methods and Techniques for Analyzing Business Competition.* New Jersey: Prentice Hall.

and ensuring that common mistakes or biases in decision-making have been avoided. Some checkpoints include:

- Identifying all assumptions made in the analysis and comparing these assumptions with case facts and external data sources to ensure that they are necessary and reasonable[3]
- Ensuring that all "facts" have been verified and opinions (given in the case and your own) have been tested against other data
- Examining the list of alternatives for possible inclusions or exclusions driven by biases or stereotypes about how things "should" be
- Checking to ensure that the use of data has not been biased to support a preferred alternative

There are both individual and group blind spots. You should examine the group process (if used during brainstorming or if the report is being prepared by a group) and the decision making of individuals to ensure that common biases have not occurred, such as:

- Group think — the tendency for groups to develop a consensus that encourages ignoring contrary evidence. This is driven by group processes that encourage compliance with group norms, and is exacerbated when the group is homogeneous and insulated from external reality checks. The nominal group technique described under brainstorming, above, is one approach to reducing the likelihood of this problem.

- Escalating commitment — the tendency to commit further resources to a decision although evidence suggests that the decision was wrong. This is an issue in case analysis when you commit to a recommendation prior to doing a thorough analysis. This premature commitment can bias the interpretation of information (framing effects), restrict the search for disconfirming evidence (confirmation bias) and limit the alternatives that are considered.

- Hindsight bias — the tendency to view evidence from the perspective of known outcomes. This is particularly an issue in case analysis if the company is real and the case historical. This allows you to see what decision-makers did and/or to see how uncertain future events developed. Your analysis of the case must focus on the facts known at the time the decision needed to be made.

---

[3] See Mitroff, I.I., and Emshoff, J.R. (1979) "On Strategic Assumption-Making: A Dialectical Approach to Policy and Planning". *The Academy of Management Review* V4 N1: 1–12

Ladder of Inference

Blind spot analysis covers much of the same ground as the "ladder of inference" shown in Figure 23.[4] The ladder of inference reminds us that our choice of actions (the recommendation in case analysis) is premised on our beliefs about the world, which are based on the conclusions we draw from our observations about the world. The raw data about the world on which we base our conclusions, however, is selectively perceived, and we make assumptions as we transform data into information.

The ladder of inference is used as an audit procedure of the process leading to a conclusion. Specifically, the ladder of inference reminds us to identify and challenge the assumptions we make to interpret data, and to ensure that we have not focused on a sub-set of the available information that could have biased our analysis.

Sensitivity Analysis

An important step prior to making a recommendation is to do a sensitivity analysis. There are two levels to this analysis. First, the blind spot analysis will identify key areas (assumptions, biases in the use of data) where judgement has been used that might affect the analysis. The blind

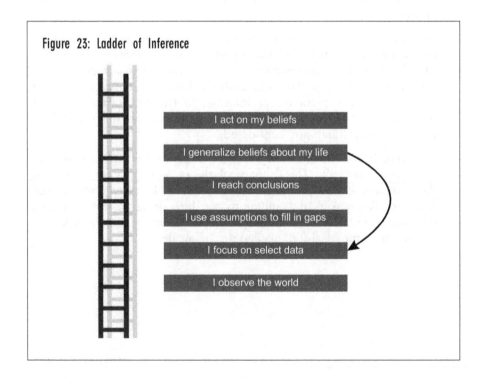

Figure 23: Ladder of Inference

I act on my beliefs

I generalize beliefs about my life

I reach conclusions

I use assumptions to fill in gaps

I focus on select data

I observe the world

---

[4] The ladder of inference is based on Senge, P., (1990). *The Fifth Discipline: The Art and Practice of the Learning Organization.* New York: Doubleday Currency.

spot analysis seeks to ensure that the assumptions and use of data are reasonable, but sensitivity analysis asks a slightly different question. If your data or assumptions are wrong, would it affect your recommendation? If large changes in assumptions do not affect the recommendation, then your recommendation is robust and you should have faith in it. On the other hand, if relatively small changes in assumptions or data (e.g., an inflation rate, or interest rate) result in large swings in your recommendation, then the confidence in your recommendation is limited by your confidence in your assumption/data. At a minimum, your write-up should alert readers to the effect of these variables on your analysis.

There are standard techniques for sensitivity analysis and dealing with uncertainty in most fields ranging from scenario analysis in strategy to simulations and expected value models in finance. A common approach in case analysis is to examine two or three levels (e.g., a base-line, pessimistic and optimistic assumption) on key variables and follow through the effect on the analysis of these different levels of key variables. Depending on the reporting format, these variations in the results may be reported as a way of reinforcing the credibility of your recommendation.

A second level of sensitivity analysis concerns the evaluation of alternatives. The decision matrix and other approaches to multi-attribute decision-making may be sensitive to the ranking process. For example, one concern in the theoretical literature is that an irrelevant alternative included in the ranking may change the way in which other alternatives are compared (this has been raised particularly with regard to the analytic hierarchy process). But more commonly, the decision matrix is created by subjectively assigning a rating on an attribute to an alternative. If you varied these ratings by one category in either direction, would this affect the ranking of alternatives? If so, then we need to look very carefully at how these ranks are assigned (e.g., in groups perhaps each member can assign ranks independently, and the rankings can be compared and reconciled).

Validation

The process of validation is a check of the recommendation against the objectives of the decision-maker and other stakeholders in the case. In practice this would involve presenting a recommendation to stakeholders to seek affirmation of the course of action. In case analysis this has to be done through a logical comparison of the likely outcomes of implementing the recommendation against the objectives and values of stakeholders. This analysis may indicate ways in which stakeholders may react to the recommendation that require either specific implementation processes or reconsideration of the recommendation, or both.

Validation is also obtained through a "gut" test of the recommendation. Everything up to this point is based on a logical analysis of the case, its issues and alternatives. If you have immersed yourself in the case and have sufficient experience with decision-making, then you may have formed a tacit understanding of the right actions. A final test is to see if that tacit understanding is consistent with what your analysis is telling you. If your "gut" suggests a different course of action, then you need to clarify why that discrepancy occurred. Perhaps your intuition is based on some factor that has not been incorporated into the analysis, or perhaps you are uncomfortable with some of the assumptions that have been made. An intuitive perspective on your results should not be enough to make you contradict your analysis, but it should be taken seriously enough to audit the results and identify any areas where small changes might affect the recommendation.

If your recommendation passes these final audits of the quality of your analysis and the likelihood of success of implementation of your recommendation, then you are ready to prepare your analysis for submission.

Recommendations and Implementation Plans

The requirements of most cases will ask you to evaluate the decision made by management in the case or to suggest a course of action for management. The recommendation will emerge from your analysis and can be justified based on that analysis. In some cases the requirements will include putting forward a plan for implementation. A useful way of thinking about implementation is in terms of the plan-do-check-act (PDCA) cycle, illustrated in Figure 24. Implementation requires considering how the recommendation should be put into action given the specific context of the case. The PDCA cycle is intended to ensure that the implementation process achieves the objectives of the decision-maker and puts in place procedures to monitor and adapt the recommendation based on any contingencies encountered.

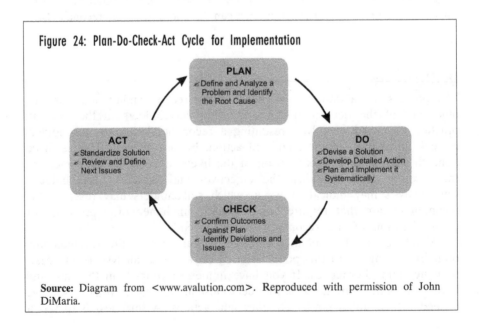

Figure 24: Plan-Do-Check-Act Cycle for Implementation

PLAN
 Define and Analyze a Problem and Identify the Root Cause

DO
 Devise a Solution
 Develop Detailed Action
 Plan and Implement it Systematically

CHECK
 Confirm Outcomes Against Plan
 Identify Deviations and Issues

ACT
 Standardize Solution
 Review and Define Next Issues

Source: Diagram from <www.avalution.com>. Reproduced with permission of John DiMaria.

An implementation plan will include the following components:

- Scoping (i.e., specifying what will be included in the implementation and what is not included)
- Specifying what resources will be needed to implement the plan and how these resources will be obtained (resources may include human and financial capital, technology etc.)
- Developing a timeline for implementing specific actions
- A plan for monitoring and evaluating the implementation to ensure that the timeline is maintained and the objectives are achieved.

Writing a Case Analysis

The format of your case analysis will be specified in the "required" section of the case assignment. It may be a short memo that highlights the essential aspects of your analysis, a letter to communicate your findings to clients, or a comprehensive report that will be used to brief others who are responsible for making a decision based on your recommendation. Regardless of the format, your case write-up should be concise, well organized, logical, and persuasive.[5] Remember that the point of your analysis is to encourage others to act on your recommendation. In general, a persuasive case write-up will demonstrate a tight connection between your recommendation and the available evidence. It should also demonstrate that you understand the objectives of the decision-maker and make a clear link between the actions you recommend and those objectives.

There are thus four key components to your case write-up: the medium (memo, letter or report), the audience (understanding who they are and their objectives), the message (the connection between your write-up and the effort you have put into the analysis, your use of evidence and reason) and you as the communicator (your credibility, eloquence and authority as a case analyst) (see Figure 25). All four elements must be aligned to make your communication persuasive.

Memo

A memo, or memorandum, is used to communicate between people in the same organization. This form of communication is typically less formal and shorter than a letter or report. A memo is concise, coherent, and sharply focused. It should include a brief introduction to frame the subject of the memo, a paragraph or paragraphs providing the body of the message, and, where appropriate, a brief conclusion. The conclusion may offer further help or contact information or simply a courteous goodbye.

---

[5] For a more comprehensive guide see May, C., and May, G.S. (1996). *Effective Writing: A Handbook for Accountants*, 4th edition. Upper Saddle River, NJ: Prentice Hall; and Ellet, W. (2007). *The Case Study Handbook. How to Read, Discuss, and Write Persuasively About Cases*. Boston: Harvard Business Press.

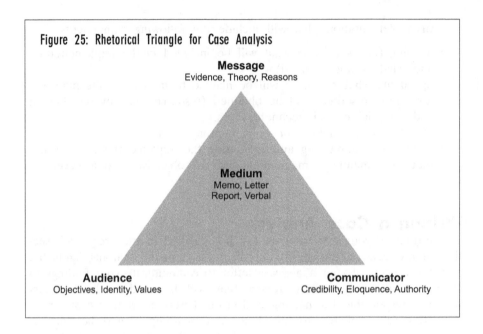

Figure 25: Rhetorical Triangle for Case Analysis

Message
Evidence, Theory, Reasons

Medium
Memo, Letter
Report, Verbal

Audience
Objectives, Identity, Values

Communicator
Credibility, Eloquence, Authority

Memos (and letters) are the preferred format for case-based examinations, since they can be prepared within the time constraints of an examination process, whereas a report, described below, requires more descriptive material concerning the case analysis process than can reasonably be written during a limited examination timeframe.

An example of a case analysis presented in memo form is included in Appendix D: Fairy Falls (Hypothetical Case: With Annotated Solution). The memo is annotated to show how the process of analysis is reflected in the memo. These annotations, of course, would not be part of the memo itself.

Letter

A letter is a memo directed to people outside the organization. Since it is addressed to clients or written on behalf of clients, its tone tends to be more formal. Since it may be addressed to someone without technical knowledge of the subject, great care must be taken to avoid jargon and to ensure that the meaning is unambiguous. In a memo or letter you need to communicate persuasively to ensure that your message is acted on. In a professional context, persuasion focuses on building credibility by providing a summary of your analysis process and including key analytic metrics in your memo or letter. (For example, providing details of the costs and benefits of key alternatives, and disclosing how these costs and benefits were estimated, and the reliability of those estimates.)

Report

Reports are used to communicate a comprehensive analysis of a case. Typically a report will include a letter (or memo) of transmittal that alerts the reader to the purpose of the report and its main conclusions or recommendations. A report's structure depends on its length and complexity, but a fairly long report typically contains a contents list, an executive summary, and an introduction, body, and conclusions. As appropriate, the report may include appendices (typically for illustrative data or detailed calculations that would reduce the body text's readability if it were included there), a bibliography, and any figures or graphics to which the body text refers. The body of the report should provide enough detail that the reader can understand the logic and analysis that supports the development of alternatives and its recommendations or conclusions.

What to Look For in a Good Case Analysis

Before leaving this chapter I want to stress once more that this guide to case analysis is not a checklist to be applied mechanically. Simply having headings that cover all the items discussed above and presenting your analysis in the format specified in the "required" section of the case will not make it a good case analysis. This guide reflects a set of principles about case analysis. A good case analysis is sensitive to the facts of the case; it interprets those facts using sound knowledge, identifies and prioritizes the issues facing the decision maker, creatively constructs and justifies alternatives, provides a recommendation based on a careful assessment of the costs and benefits of each alternative, and provides guidance for implementing the recommendation. A good case write-up provides evidence of the analysis process that you followed, and is written clearly and persuasively. Doing a good case analysis — in fact, doing a sound analysis of any business decision — is not easy! It requires a set of skills that must be honed by practice and exercised with diligence and creativity. You will be able to develop these skills by using this book.

Chapter Summary

Making a recommendation in case analysis requires that you be sure that this is the right recommendation and that it be communicated persuasively. The quality of your recommendation can be tested by auditing the process by which your decision was made, and ensuring that it has not been inadvertently influenced by hidden assumptions or failures of inference. It is also worthwhile to think through how each stakeholder in the case might react to the recommendation if it was implemented. This may raise additional issues that can be addressed through advice on implementation. Finally, your recommendation needs to be communicated persuasively; the point of your analysis is to get people to act. This requires knowing your audience and presenting the recommendation in a way that the audience can understand and value. We focus on written communication, and examine different formats of a case write-up for different audiences; the next Chapter looks at case analysis in real time face-to-face settings.

Problems

1. Discuss the necessary steps to take in Blind Spot Analysis.

2. Explain the main purpose of conducting a sensitivity analysis.

3. Summarize each step of the "Plan, Do, Check, Act" cycle for implementation.

4. Compare and contrast the form and purposes of a memo, letter, and report as the output of a case analysis.

Exercises

1. Prepare a report on the Appendix C: Eisner's Mousetrap (Disney) for the Board of Directors. After you have completed your report, prepare a letter to shareholders and an internal memo to Eisner. Focus on how the audience and medium change the way you present your message.

2. Identify the key differences between blind spot analysis, sensitivity analysis and validation processes in case analysis. Which aspect of the case analysis process is the focus of each of these procedures?

3. Review Appendix D: Fairy Falls (Hypothetical Case: With Annotated Solution). Identify the key elements of the implementation plan in this case. Is the implementation plan complete? Specify any additional aspects of the implementation plan that are necessary to complete the plan.

8 Working with Others on Case Analyses

It is common to use group work for various aspects of case analysis. These may be discussion groups formed to allow you an intimate context in which to share your ideas and expand your perspective on the case, or groups formed to actually do the case analysis and submit a report. Effective groups can contribute both to the learning experience and to the quality of case analyses, but making groups effective requires work. It is important to understand the norms for group interactions that will help improve group outcomes, and to understand the skills that you will develop by participating in group case discussions.

I begin this Chapter focusing on techniques to improve the effectiveness of case analysis groups, and then change the focus to case discussions in the classroom. In case based learning, a complete process involves individual study of the case, group discussions and analysis, and ends with a discussion in the classroom. Each component of the process will add to your understanding of the case and the lessons you will draw from the experience.

Norms for Group Work

Students often do case analyses in groups or teams. This approach to case analysis provides you with practice with the problem-solving approach that is typically used in business — cross-functional teams are brought together to deal with key problems. When a team functions effectively, it generates better alternatives and makes better recommendations than an individual can. When a team does not function effectively, it can be a frustrating and emotionally draining experience. Here are some guidelines for helping your team to produce an excellent case report:

1. Be prepared. Every member of the group must have done his/her reading and come to the group meeting prepared to participate.

2. Take responsibility. To use legal language, every member of the group is "joint and severally liable" for the outcome. In other

words, every individual is responsible for the entire project. This has implications that are spelled out below. The group must establish very early what it expects of its members. If problems arise, they should be discussed and resolved within the group. (This means moving the group to a higher level of functioning, not sweeping problems under the rug or reducing the team to a series of individual tasks.)

3. Challenge one another. Although it may be convenient to assign tasks to different members of the group, you are responsible for the quality of the work done. All members must be willing to challenge one another (a) to ensure that each understands all the work that was done by the others, and (b) to be satisfied that the work meets everyone's standard of excellence. The final product must be a seamless report, not simply a merged set of individual documents. As a member of the team, you should be prepared to answer questions about any aspect of the final report, regardless of your specific contributions.

4. Practise active listening. To work effectively together, the team members must practise active listening skills. This means being open to others' opinions and respectful of differences; it also involves all the individual members providing feedback to demonstrate that they understand other members' positions and that everyone has been heard. When giving feedback, be specific and provide examples, and do so in a mutually supportive way, without being competitive or aggressive.

One of the most common complaints about group work is that there is "free riding" by some members of the group: i.e., taking credit for the work without doing a fair share of that work. The norms described above are, in part, designed to overcome this problem. Some other techniques for dealing with this issue include:

1. Writing motivational contracts. These contracts will specify the norms of the group and allow for penalty clauses, such as changes in the distribution of the grade among group members or even expulsion from the group. These penalty clauses require some form of mutual assessment within the group and the cooperation of the instructor in enforcing the contract. The contract may also be enforceable through peer pressure and counselling when groups fail to correct the behaviour of a free rider within the group.

2. The stepladder technique. This technique forms a core group for each task.[1] In order to become a member of the core group, each individual must do their own preparation and present this work to

---

[1] Rogelberg, S.G., Barnes-Farrell, J.L., and Lowe, C.A. (1992). "The stepladder technique: An alternative group structure facilitating effective group decision making", *Journal of Applied Psychology*, 77(5), 730–737.

the group. The group then builds on the individual contributions and reaches a group consensus on the final product.

3. Maintaining work logs. In combination with motivational contracts, one way to fight freeriding is to raise the visibility of individual contributions by keeping work logs that detail who did what within a group. These logs are particularly useful if the group signs off on the quality of the work done rather than focusing simply on task completion.

Group work is intended to improve the quality of case reports and the quality of the learning experience. It does so by exposing students to other perspectives and by encouraging them to develop key skills (such as leadership and follower skills, communication and negotiation skills, and organizational skills). Group work may not be the most efficient way to complete a task. It is used when the objective is to improve the quality of the work, not to get it done in the least amount of time. If your instructor has assigned a group case analysis, his/her expectations for the quality of the work will be higher than had the analysis been done by individuals. Keep this in mind!

Cases in the Classroom

Even if you are using cases without being assigned to a group, you may want to consider forming a group to talk about the case prior to discussion in the classroom. Several of the stages of case analysis discussed above are enhanced by using group processes (notably issue identification, alternative generation and post-analysis audit processes). Your learning will be maximized by engaging in individual, group and class discussions (see Figure 26).

Case Discussions in the Classroom

In the literature on academic course design there is a distinction between the "curriculum", the "adjacent curriculum" and the "hidden curriculum." The curriculum is the material that is listed in the syllabus and is the focus of our day-to-day interactions in the classroom. The adjacent curriculum is the set of norms and rules that are used to run the classroom and must be known to students so that they can function effectively within the wider educational organization. These are norms concerning things, such as being on time, not using your cell phone during class, and the due dates and format for deliverables that will be graded during the term. The hidden curriculum is the set of skills that students will gain by participating in the course without realizing explicitly that the process is part of their education. Case discussions are part of all three aspects of the curriculum.

Obviously, a case is assigned to explore and develop your understanding of the issues involved in a particular situation. The cases have been chosen by your instructor as part of an explicit curriculum. The discussion

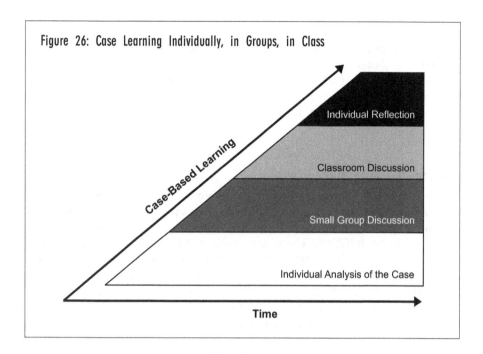

Figure 26: Case Learning Individually, in Groups, in Class

Case-Based Learning

Individual Reflection

Classroom Discussion

Small Group Discussion

Individual Analysis of the Case

Time

of the case, however, has its own purpose: a hidden curriculum that is very important to what you will take away from the class. You discuss the case to:

- practice skills in persuasive oral communications
- develop active listening skills
- gain an appreciation for the diversity of views held by your peers, in particular the diversity that stems from different cultural backgrounds, prior education and experience.

In order to successfully experience this hidden curriculum, your instructor needs to create an adjacent curriculum, i.e., a set of rules and norms, which will guide the discussion process.

Creating a Safe Environment for Case Discussions

In order to maximize participation in a case discussion, everyone must feel "safe" to participate. This is not an issue of physical safety, but a matter of trust and respect. Your instructor should spend some time outlining the norms for your discussions; if this does not happen, then you may wish to raise the issue. Some basic norms that most groups will adopt are:

- all interactions among group members are to be polite and respectful
- there should be no personal comments
- there should be no profanity
- all members should recognize and respect religious and ethnic differences

- Each person has a right to be heard and understood
- No one person should dominate the discussion
- No one should be interrupted while speaking (although the discussion leader may ask for clarification or, in the interests of time, ask for a brief summary of the point)
- Minority opinions are to be encouraged and expressed

Directing the Case Discussion

The case discussion leader, whether this is your instructor or another student in the class, has the important role of directing the discussion. This is a subtle process and must be handled skillfully in order for the case discussion to be fulfilling. There are three main roles: (1) managing the order in which case material is discussed, (2) managing the flow of the discussion of each issue, and (3) ensuring that the discussion covers all of the important issues. It is important to note that in implementing these roles, the discussion leader is not trying to achieve a predetermined outcome; each role is concerned with the **process** of discussion, as explained below.

The order in which the case is discussed is important. Typically the discussion will begin with a discussion of the facts of the case. This is to ensure that everyone in the class agrees on the context in which the case occurs and the relevant facts that must be considered as the discussion moves forward. Many students want to jump straight to the analysis and recommendations, believing that the "facts" are obvious — resist this temptation! You may be surprised that different people in the room will see the same "facts" in different ways. This is because we respond to the meaning of events and objects, and not just their physical appearance. So we may all agree that there was a disagreement between two actors in the case but some people may see this as a normal part of business interactions, while others may see it as a serious breakdown of the culture of the organization. These differences in interpretation need to be explored before moving to the analysis of issues within the case.

As the discussion of the case develops, the discussion leader's main role is to manage the discussion process to ensure that everyone has an opportunity to participate and that the discussion moves to an appropriate depth. In some cases the discussion leader will simply recognize the next speaker to give them the floor. In other cases, the discussion leader may encourage a debate between two people in the class in order to explore an issue that has prompted divergent views. On occasion the leader may pose questions to push the analysis deeper into the case, or refer back to an earlier comment that highlights a distinction that needs to be explored. Some leaders will "cold call" students to encourage them to participate in the discussion (and prevent them from falling asleep).

A well written case allows for a rich exploration of alternatives and sometimes the debate on a particular issue can so engage the group that time management becomes an issue. The discussion leader will have identified certain issues that they believe are important to discuss. (This is not to suggest that additional issues may not arise during the discussion.) Given the limits of a normal class period, the leader must watch the clock and decide when to move on to the next issue in the case. Do not take this as a sign that the issue under discussion is less important, or that the discussion was "wrong" in any sense. Remember that the point to the case discussion is to bring out the richness of the issues. You and your classmates will have further opportunities after the class to carry on with any discussions that you would like to explore further.

Strategies for Participating in Case Discussions

The most important thing that you should know about case discussions is that the discussion leader wants you to participate in the discussion! In spite of this many students feel reluctant to participate or find it difficult to join in spirited debates in a case class because of language concerns or learning style differences, as outlined in Chapter 2: Learning Styles and Case Learning. This can adversely affect your learning in the class, the opportunities of other members of the class to gain from your insights, and your grade in the course where participation is included as part of the evaluation. You need to develop strategies to overcome these issues. Here are some basic suggestions:

- Be prepared! You will not feel comfortable participating if you have not read and thought about the case. It is often useful to prepare by yourself and then discuss the case in a small group before the actual case discussion to give you the confidence to participate in the larger setting.

- If you are hesitant to jump into the middle of the discussion, make sure that you contribute when the instructor asks for opinions and inputs. For example, the instructor may ask for someone to highlight the basic facts or to identify a new issue. If you have prepared the case in advance, these will be good opportunities for you to make a contribution to the discussion.

- Follow the discussion carefully and look for:
  o Statements made by your classmates with which you disagree; be prepared to make your point based on analysis and case facts.
  o Opportunities to refine and deepen the analysis being discussed, particularly where you can relate the analysis to the specifics of the case.
  o Related issues that affect the issue at the core of the current discussion. In many situations, issues are not independent, and analysis and recommendations that focus on one issue may prove inappropriate when considered in conjunction with other issues.

The discussion of a case is an important part of your learning experience. Remember that the <u>process</u> of case discussion is as important as the <u>con-</u>

tent of case discussion. Use the case discussion to develop your communications and active listening skills. The role of the discussion leader is to direct the flow of the discussion, to ensure that the depth and breadth of discussion is appropriate, and to encourage wide participation among your classmates. You can contribute to the quality of case discussions by adopting these as your personal goals.

Case Presentations

The commentary of the previous section applies to case presentations as well as discussion. Although you may be asked to "present" the case, you are really being asked to lead a discussion. Your presentation should provide a structure within which the discussion can occur. For example, you may want to spend a few minutes reviewing the key case facts and then invite discussion: do people agree that you have identified the key facts; is you interpretation of their significance consistent with others' views? Typically a case presentation will spend most of the allotted time on your identification of issues, alternatives and your recommendation. The latter two items are likely to be the "value added" in your presentation.

Straw Polls

One way that the presenters can engage the audience in a case presentation is to use straw polls (votes) at key points in the discussion. Votes allow the audience to express their opinions on the prioritization of issues and the evaluation of alternatives. It provides the presenting group with some "buy in" to their analysis that helps engage the audience. The danger, of course, is that the straw polls will suggest a different way forward than that prepared by the presenters. This should be treated as an opportunity to deepen the discussion. It may reflect different degrees of engagement and depth of analysis between the audience and the presenters, but one should never underestimate the "wisdom of crowds." The majority may have a good idea that you wish to explore further.

Challenge/Management Teams

One variation on the presentation format is to assign two teams to the analysis and presentation of the case. One team acts as a consultant and prepares the analysis and recommendation; the other team acts as the decision-maker to whom the recommendation is presented. The challenge team's role is to ensure that the analysis and recommendation presented is defensible and consistent with the decision-maker's objectives. They should not focus on minor details of the presentation, but should provide a perspective that ensures that the discussion is focused on meeting the client's needs.

Chapter Summary

Your learning with cases begins with individual study, is extended through small group work and culminates with the discussion in the classroom. Group work and class discussion require particular skills to ensure that everyone benefits. When working with groups, ensure that everyone knows and agrees to the norms by which the group will operate. Some basic norms for group work are: be prepared, take responsibility, challenge one another and practise active listening. The classroom allows you and your group to present your perspective on the case, to challenge others and to finalize your views. Go into a classroom discussion with well-prepared positions and a willingness to change your mind. Your participation in groups and the classroom is likely to be affected by your learning style. Understanding that style will let you chose ways of participating that are most comfortable to you and productive to others.

Problems

1. List four guidelines that every group (and group member) should follow in order to conduct a successful case analysis.

2. Outline some techniques that can be used to deal with "free-riders".

3. Discuss some of the basic norms that are generally adopted by effective case discussion groups.

4. What should you specifically look for when trying to have effective participation in a class or a group discussion?

Exercises

1. Assume the role of the management of JetBlue receiving the report of a consulting team. The required part of this case is the preparation of an analysis of the event and a plan for action. What questions would you ask to probe for the depth of the analysis presented? What criteria would you use to evaluate the quality of the report presented?

2. Prepare a motivational contract for group work. What are the things that you expect of group members? How will you monitor these behaviours? What incentives will you provide for positive contributions to the functioning of the group? Does your contract include process and outcome measures/rewards?

3. Identify:
   (a) Ways that you could encourage others to participate in case discussions.
   (b) Ways to test whether or not you have understood what others say during a case discussion (active listening).

Chapter Summary

Problems

Exercises

9 Case-Based Examinations

As mentioned in the introduction, cases are frequently used in professional examinations and, of course, as examinations in case-based courses leading to managerial and professional careers. Writing case-based examinations uses all of the skills discussed above, but with time constraints and space limited reporting formats. In this chapter I will provide an overview of the case grading process to highlight what graders are looking for, and then return to the process of writing case exams.

Grading Case-Based Examinations

You might ask: "If there are truly no right answers in case-based examinations, then how can they be graded?" It is challenging for instructors to grade case based examinations, but some common practices have developed that are useful to understand if you are writing a case-based examination.

First, the grading scheme for case based examinations is likely to have redundant grades; that is, there will be more grades available than the worth of the case-based question. For example, if a case is graded out of 100, the grading key may list 400 points available! This is because it is unlikely that any candidate will cover every possibility in their analysis, but a good analysis can be performed without touching on every possibility. The available grades will also depend on a sequence of issues/ alternatives/ recommendations. Different sequences may be regarded as equally valid, but it would be unlikely (and unwise) if a student tried to follow through in detail each possible sequence. Another trick that graders use (primarily with new cases) is to do a test marking of a random sample of exams, and to develop the grading scheme based on the set of issues and alternatives seen in that test group. In other words, case grading relies heavily on peer comparisons or benchmarking (relative performance) rather than on a predetermined standard.

Second, the grading scheme is more likely to have detailed grades available for the early stages of the case analysis. For example, while the grader can reasonably anticipate the issues that will be seen in the case, it is less likely that the grader can anticipate every alternative that candidates may develop. So the grader may expect to see certain basic technical analyses being done to identify issues, or to see certain high priority issues identified and have clear grades for these sections. Later sections of the analysis may attract as high a weight in the grading scheme but the grades for these sections will be more student centered.

Third, the grading scheme is likely to move from a content focus to a logic or process focus for the later portions of the case analysis. In other words, after you have demonstrated that you understand the case and identified the key issues, the grader then focuses on your justification for your prioritization of issues and whether or not your alternatives and recommendations actually address the issues that you have prioritized. The majority of grades are available for a logically integrated, coherent and comprehensive analysis.

Finally, case based examinations are typically graded to reflect a range of results rather than a specific numeric result. For example, the Chartered Accountant's UFE is graded according to five levels of demonstrated competency: not addressed, nominal competency, reaching competency, competent and highly competent.[1] The use of these types of ranges for addressing performance on case exams allows for multiple ways of demonstrating competence and for the professional judgment of graders in assessing the competency of exam writers.

In professional exams the knowledge that you are expected to have is specified in "competency maps" that should be available from the professional association setting the exam. These competency maps can be thought of as the things that any competent case analyst/practitioner should know and be able to apply during the exam. The actual case used in the exam will draw on situations where some sub-sample of the skills reflected in the competency map will help to identify issues, generate alternatives and make recommendations. Candidates must demonstrate that they can recognize when certain knowledge should be applied, and apply that knowledge appropriately to the case facts.

The Canadian Chartered Accountants' Uniform Final Evaluation (UFE), for example, grades case analyses (which they refer to as "simulations") on three criteria: sufficiency, depth and breadth of knowledge.[2] The case analyst must demonstrate competence on all basic dimensions of the competency map; this is referred to as sufficiency. The case analyst must also demonstrate depth of knowledge on areas of specific concern within a case. For the CAs this requires a deep understanding of performance measurement and assurance. Finally, the case analyst must demonstrate breadth of knowledge across all of the competencies that are needed to do a comprehensive case analysis. This means that you cannot

---

[1] "The grading game" *CA Magazine* April 2006.

[2] From <http://www.cica.ca/become-a-ca/documents/item9612.pdf>

omit areas and attempt to compensate with a deeper application of the knowledge that you are comfortable with (so that class you slept through will come back to haunt you!).

Professional case examinations are graded by teams of graders drawn from practice. The perspective brought to the grading is thus what a competent practitioner would have done in the circumstances with the facts and time available. The grading team will typically begin by grading a sample of the examinations and comparing notes. This part of the process serves two purposes: the test grading helps refine the grading key to allow the graders expertise to be brought into the process, and the test grading ensures that each grader is using the same standard when grading the exam. As the grading progresses though the bulk of the exams, grading team leaders will do re-grades of random exams to ensure that the grading process is reliable, and will be available to reconcile any issues that arise. Grading professional examinations is a significant undertaking that is treated very seriously.

Writing Case-Based Exams

Writing a case-based examination is challenging. You may be stressed, and feel overwhelmed by the scope of the task and the lack of guidance. If you have been practicing the skills in this book, however, you will be ready. The main issue is to ensure that you work systematically through the process. In particular, make sure that you allow sufficient time to do a detailed reading of the case and make notes about context, issues, facts, objectives and constraints. A crucial part of the question is the "required" section that specifies what the examiner is looking for both in terms of substance (e.g., a recommendation, an analysis of alternatives etc.) and in terms of form (e.g., a letter, a memo, etc.). Make sure that you have a firm grasp of the requirements of the examination before proceeding any further — the best quality work focused on the wrong requirement is still a failure.

Remember that the requirement may suggest a particular form of output but this does not mean that you start with that output. You must do your own work before you are ready to present your results, and you must have done the work in order to professionally justify your recommendation. So work through the process of identifying issues and prioritizing these issues. Your presentation will have to justify why you have chosen to focus on some issues rather than others, so make sure that you have well developed reasons (based on analysis) for your choices. Develop a set of alternatives (even though you may not report on all the alternatives you have considered) and evaluate those alternatives based on criteria that are tied to the objectives of the decision-maker.

Given the approach to grading professional exams noted above, present your work in a clear, well organized manner that facilitates grading. (Graders are working under time pressures too, and they will not be able to read between the lines or guess what you intended to say — be explicit.) Your work should strive to demonstrate your knowledge. If you are making a recommendation, the grader is not interested in your opinions. They are looking for the use of analytic tools and professional knowledge that justifies a recommendation.

Although the grading schemes for professional case analyses include both breadth and depth criteria, you should avoid "memory dumps." There is nothing more frustrating to a case grader than to see good ideas buried in a pile of trivia. This approach to exam writing demonstrates that the case writer does not have the confidence and maturity to focus on the key issues in a case and, instead, provides a scattering of ideas with the hope that the grader will give you the benefit of the doubt. They won't. Case examinations focus on the ability to apply knowledge, not just the possession of knowledge. The point of this type of examination is to ensure that you have the higher level cognitive skills to enter practice, and to provide a standard of service and care to clients that justifies them placing their fate in your hands.

Chapter Summary

Case examinations are used to test your case analysis abilities and to demonstrate that you have the ability to apply substantive knowledge to complex and ambiguous situations. Professional entrance examinations, in particular, are looking for you to demonstrate that you have the knowledge and skills to handle the types of problems routinely seen in practice. Professional examination graders are looking for evidence that you have both the depth and breadth of knowledge expected of entry level practitioners, but beyond this they are looking for evidence that you can choose when particular knowledge should be applied and can vary how knowledge is used in specific circumstances. When writing case exams, ensure that you provide a coherent and well organized answer that demonstrates these skills, and makes it easy for graders to see that you have followed a sound process leading to your recommendation.

Problems

1. Why do case-examination marking schemes have redundant grades?

2. What is the relationship between professional "competency maps" and case-based examinations?

3. Identify three reasons why your answers to case-based examinations should be concise and well-focused.

Exercises

1. Identify one or more professional associations that use case based examinations and review the example examinations and solutions that are provided (for example, CPA Ireland provides an extensive list of past examinations and suggested solutions at <http://www.cpaireland.ie/displaycontent.aspx?node=98&groupID=98&parentID=3>.) Compare the suggested solutions with the suggestions for exam writing provided in this chapter.

2. On your next case assignment, exchange your case write-up with a colleague and provide feedback on your colleague's work according to the norms summarized in this chapter. The process of evaluating another's case write-up will help you to understand the attributes of a good case analysis and how presentation skills facilitate giving feedback.

10 Epilogue

Learning to analyze cases takes time and practice. In one sense, doing case analysis is a very natural activity. Each day we encounter complex, ambiguous situations and react to them without much conscious thought. This natural sense of reacting to cases, unfortunately, may blind us to the fact that we really don't do it very well or that we could do it better by being more systematic in how we go about case analysis. For some people who encounter cases, their first reaction is, "This is easy!" Chances are they are unconsciously incompetent (see Figure 27), unaware of their own limitations. Part of the objective of this book is to raise your level of consciousness, to make you aware of alternative ways of doing case analysis

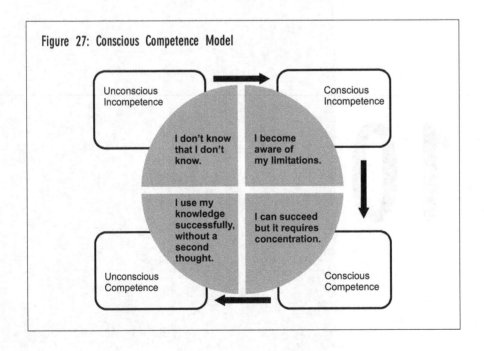

Figure 27: Conscious Competence Model

and of the techniques to help you be systematic in your approach. With luck, you are now consciously incompetent. While this may not sound like a good thing, being consciously incompetent means that you will not make blind mistakes; you will recognize when you need help and when you need to refer back to this book! Over time, with practice, you will become consciously competent. You will do high quality case analyses although you may still need to think about each step. Ultimately though, the logic explored in this book will become second nature and you will use the appropriate tools to help you without even thinking about it. You will, with practice, become unconsciously competent. Most people are still trying to get there.

This book has provided you with techniques to handle each stage in the process of case analysis. These techniques are summarized below in Table 9. Each technique has been chosen to help you implement a thorough case analysis process, and to ensure that common biases in decision-making are not affecting the way that you perceive problems and

Table 9: Summary of Techniques for Case Analysis

	Stage of Case Analysis			
	Issue Identification and Prioritization	**Alternative Generation**	**Evaluation of Alternatives**	**Making Recommendations**
Techniques and Tools	GAP Analysis	Brainstorming: Nominal group technique	Analysis of Competing Hypotheses (ACH)	Blind Spot Analysis
	Root Cause Analysis	Brainstorming: Delphi technique	Cause Mapping	Ladder of Inference
	Power of Questions Pyramid	6-Hat Method	Feasibility Analysis	Sensitivity Analysis — Assumptions
	5-Why Technique	SCAMPER technique	Dominance Analysis	Sensitivity Analysis — Evaluation Criteria
	7-S Model	Case-based reasoning	Force Field Analysis	Validation — Stakeholder reactions
	Risk Matrix	Metaphorical Reasoning	Decision Matrix	Validation — "gut" check
	Affinity Diagrams	Scenario Planning	Analytical Hierarchy	Rhetorical Triangle

opportunities, generate and evaluate alternatives, and present your recommendation to decision-makers. Remember that the key to effective case analysis is to focus on the process. If your case analysis process is thorough and unbiased, then you can have confidence in your recommendations.

Appendix A

Decision-Making Biases

Researchers have identified many biases in decision-making. Typically these biases are carefully defined to illustrate the conditions under which they occur, and researchers try not to overstate the effect of the bias or the scope of its impact on decision-making. The result is that there are dozens of named biases in the literature. The nature of the biases identified, however, do show patterns that can be summarized in ways that allow managers to be sensitized to the bias and/or to develop techniques to debias decision-making. Figure 28 shows one way of summarizing decision-making biases, published by the consulting company McKinsey as a guide to managers making strategic decisions. Another approach to categorizing the biases is shown in Table 2.

From the perspective of case analysis, four groups of bias are of particular concern:

1. Biases affecting the recognition of issues: the recognition of issues can be affected by tendencies to draw on easily visualized events, rather than seeking root causes, and the tendency to seek confirming information for our beliefs. See Chapter 4: Identifying Issues for techniques to overcome these biases.

2. Biases affecting the generation of alternatives: the range of alternatives considered can be constrained by the tendency to anchor on arbitrary starting points and seeking incremental alternatives, and by the narrowness of our personal perspectives on possibilities. See Chapter 5: Identifying Alternatives for techniques to overcome these biases.

3. Biases affecting the evaluation of alternatives: the evaluation of alternatives can be affected by our susceptibility to be concerned with sunk costs and our escalating commitment to courses of action, and by tendencies to treat gains and losses asymmetrically. See Chapter 6: Evaluating Alternatives for techniques to overcome these biases.

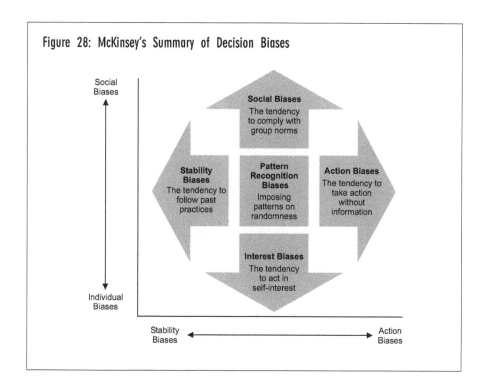

Figure 28: McKinsey's Summary of Decision Biases

4.   Biases affecting recommendations and implementation: our recommendations can be affected by tendencies to become overconfident in our decisions and to underestimate the ability of others to react to our decisions. See Chapter 7: Making Recommendations for techniques to overcome these biases.

Appendix B

JetBlue Airways' Customer Service Fiasco

For years after it was set up in 1999, JetBlue Airways had been a favorite with airline analysts. Modeled loosely on America's legendary low cost carrier Southwest Airlines, JetBlue achieved relatively quick success by bringing an element of 'coolness' to low cost travel. Unlike Southwest, which took its low cost image seriously and avoided frills altogether, JetBlue offered comforts like leather seats and seat-back televisions. The airline also flew a new fleet of Airbus A380s and Embraer-190s, and the crew was known to be cheery and helpful — seemingly, a rarity in the airline industry.

JetBlue was especially known for its commitment to customer service, and positioned itself as an airline that cared about its passengers. It was known to give away free food passes and flight tickets to passengers even when flights were delayed because of external causes that were no fault of the airline. JetBlue was also known to never cancel any of its flights, no matter what the delay, as it believed that passengers would rather get to their destinations late than never.

It was this policy that landed JetBlue in trouble in mid February 2007, when a huge snow storm affected the Northeast and Midwest regions of the US. While other airlines cancelled flights and rescheduled operations, JetBlue persisted in believing that the flights would eventually take off, and kept passengers stranded for several hours. In one extreme and well publicized instance, passengers were stranded on board a plane on the tarmac at New York's JFK airport for nearly 11 hours. Eventually however, the airline was forced to cancel most of its flights.

However, even after the storm cleared JetBlue struggled to get back on its feet as the cancelled flights had played havoc with its systems which were not equipped to deal with cancellations. The airline's poor database management systems also resulted in major problems in tracking and lining up pilots and flight crew who were within federal regulation limits for the number of flying hours to operate the resumed flights. In addition to this, the delays and cancellations had caused a baggage crisis with several passengers finding their luggage missing.

It took several days for JetBlue's operations to smoothen, and the airline was forced to cancel nearly 1,200 flights in all in the days following the storm. Meanwhile, airlines like American Airlines, Continental Airlines and Delta Airways, which had cancelled flights immediately were able to resume operations more quickly. Within days after the fiasco, JetBlue's founder and CEO David Neeleman unveiled a 'Customer Bill of Rights', which laid out the airline's policy towards compensating passengers for delays and cancellations. JetBlue also created a new position of Chief Operations Officer, appointing Russell Chew, a former COO at the U.S. Federal Aviation Administration to the post. Additionally, JetBlue launched a new database management system to help it track crew and baggage better.

The fiasco reportedly cost JetBlue $30 million, and was expected to affect the company's financial position adversely. JetBlue had been grappling with financial difficulties (mainly because of a sharp rise in fuel prices) since 2005, after years of spectacular growth. Notwithstanding financial losses, the loss of goodwill was expected to be much more serious for the airline.

Some analysts observed that Neeleman and JetBlue should be commended for accepting blame and trying to make amends. Others however were skeptical about whether any of the remedial steps would actually help the airline regain favor with passengers.

Additional Readings and References

1. "JetBlue Apologizes after Passengers Stranded," <www.msnbc.msn.com>, February 16, 2007.
2. Larry Dignan, "JetBlue Fiasco: A Database Could Have Made a Difference," www.zdnet.com, February 20, 2007.
3. Bachman, J. "JetBlue's Fiasco Could Improve Flying," *BusinessWeek*, February 21, 2007.
4. McGregor, J. "Customer Service Champs," *BusinessWeek*, March 5, 2007. <http://www.businessweek.com/pdf/270529bwEprint.pdf>
5. "JetBlue Adds Operations Chief after Service Fiasco," Reuters, March 7, 2007.
6. "JetBlue Airways Customer Bill of Rights," <www.jetblue.com> (accessed on April 4, 2007).

Required

Take the role of the new "Operations Chief" (a position created after the problem described in the case), and prepare a memo to the CEO providing your analysis of what happened and your recommendations for action during your first 100 days on the job.

Appendix C

Michael Eisner
at Disney

Between 1984 and 2005, Michael Eisner was the CEO of The Walt Disney Corporation. During this time Eisner oversaw major changes in the strategy of Disney, including moving into more adult film-making, expanding into television networks, including ABC and ESPN, and expanding their network of theme parks around the world. The period also saw major confrontations between Eisner and the Disney Board of Directors.

The events of this period have been well captured in:

- Chronology of the Walt Disney Company
  <http://kpolsson.com/disnehis/>
- Eisner's Mousetrap: Disney's CEO says the company has a lot of varied problems he can fix. But what if the real issue is something he can't face? By Marc Gunther (Reporter Associate Carol Vinzant) Fortune Magazine September 6, 1999
  <http://money.cnn.com/magazines/fortune/fortune_arhive/1999/09/06/265291/index.htm>
- Has Eisner Lost the Disney Magic? The company has been walloped by terror and recession. But its problems start at the top. By Marc Gunther Reporter (Associate Noshua Watson) Fortune Magazine January 7, 2002 <http://money.cnn.com/magazines/fortune/fortune_archive/2002/01/07/316039/index.htm>.

Required

Based on the articles above, as Chairman of the Board of the Walt Disney Company prepare a memo to the Board of Directors about the issues facing Disney and what can be done.

Appendix D

Fairy Falls

(Hypothetical Case:
With Annotated Solution)

THE CASE

Background

In Canada, the Constitution gives the federal and provincial governments the right to collect taxes to support their activities. The provinces, however, are restricted to "direct" taxes — that is, taxes that are paid by the person taxed and that cannot be passed on to others. This feature means that businesses cannot be taxed by the provinces in ways that are passed on to consumers. In several court cases,[1] businesses have successfully sued provincial and municipal governments (which are legal creations of the province, and hence restricted to provincial powers) when permit and licensing fees amount to more than the costs associated with providing those services. Businesses have argued that the excess of a fee over the cost of providing services constitutes an indirect tax that will be passed on to consumers and thus is unconstitutional. Past court decisions suggest that the provinces (and municipalities) must ensure that all permit and license fees reflect the actual cost of services.

Elizabeth Montgomery, the mayor of Fairy Falls,[2] a small community in northern Ontario, has been reading summaries of these court cases. Although there is not yet a provincial requirement for municipalities to change the way they set fees, she is beginning to worry that the town may be in violation of the law. In addition, the Town Council has committed

---

This chapter is based on Chapter 3, pp. 21–26 from Richardson, A.J. *Cases and Active Learning Exercises in Managerial Accounting* © 2007 Nelson Education Ltd. Reproduced by permission <www.cengage.com/permissions>.

[1] For example, *Ontario Home Builders' Association v. York Region Board of Education* [1996] 2 S.C.R. 929.

[2] This is a fictitious town and is not intended to represent real events or people. The costs shown in Table 10 are extracted based on actual practices in a number of municipalities for illustration purposes only.

itself to sound financial management practices. As one way of meeting this commitment, it wants to make sure that it stays ahead of emerging issues. Since the town issues several thousand permits and licenses each year, this could become a significant issue in the future. She has asked you, the Chief Administrative Officer (CAO), to provide an analysis and recommendation.

The Town of Fairy Falls

Fairy Falls is a small town in northern Ontario, an area characterized by small lakes, a rugged, granite-strewn landscape, and tall pines. The population is widely dispersed and consists mainly of seasonal residents. The permanent population is about 5,000, but this increases to about 50,000 during the summer months as people move into vacation homes, trailer parks, and campgrounds. This means that the demand for municipal services, including permits and licenses, varies dramatically during the year. A number of small businesses in the area (e.g., stores, motels, and fishing charters) cater to vacationers. There are also cranberry farms in the district, which are prospering. Fairy Falls is the administrative centre of this district.

The municipal office is located in a historic building in Fairy Falls that also houses a museum, as well as a visitors' centre operated by the Chamber of Commerce. The municipal operation is very lean, with the following full-time salaried personnel:

- The CAO, who also serves as economic development officer.
- The treasurer.
- The town clerk, who also serves as the municipal planner, and who issues licenses for lotteries, temporary road closings, and pits and quarries.
- The bylaw enforcement officer, who monitors permits issued and who investigates reports of violations of municipal regulations.
- The planning officer, who handles building permits, dock permits, septic permits and so on. (Additional staff is brought in during the start of the construction season to ensure that buildings are not delayed by the approvals and inspections process.)

Fire services are provided by a volunteer fire department, which has a full-time fire chief, who provides training and who ensures that the equipment is maintained. The fire chief also issues burning permits during the fire season. Policing is handled by the Ontario Provincial Police under a long-term contract with the town.

The largest department, housed in a separate facility, is Public Works, which handles road repairs and maintenance, garbage and waste treatment, and the maintenance of parks and cemeteries. This department also maintains the town's water system and ensures that provincial regulations regarding water quality are met or exceeded at all times. This department works closely with the planning officer to ensure that development permits are aligned with capital improvements to the town's infrastructure. The department has a Public Works Director and a permanent staff of five. Seasonal help is added during the summer to deal with road repairs and to provide services to seasonal residents, and during the winter to deal with snow removal. In spring and fall this department shrinks in size.

Permits and Licensing

The main permits/licenses issued by the town on a routine basis are:

- building permits,
- dock permits,
- septic permits,
- burn permits,
- lottery and Bingo licenses, and
- licenses to operate pits and quarries.

The town has never had a formal policy regarding the amounts to be charged for permits and licenses. Generally, the fees have been set by the Town Council on the recommendation of the CAO. The fees were originally set to be comparable to those of neighbouring municipalities; this was to ensure that the amounts did not impede business development. The fee increases that have been approved by the Town Council have tended to match increases in the town's overall expenditures and have averaged three percent per year over the past decade, although some fees, such as dog licenses, have not changed for a decade. Some of the fees charged are listed in Table 10.

Required

Prepare a memo to the mayor that analyzes the following:

- The town's current compliance with the court's view of appropriate permit and license fees.

- If you believe the town is not in compliance, where you believe changes should be made, and how these changes should be made.

- Any additional issues that would arise if fees were changed.

Table 10: Examples of Permit and License Fees

Purpose	Administered by	Fee Charged	Comments
Cemetery	Planning Officer	• $500 per grave plot; • internment $600 (winter internment $800)	Lifetime maintenance of the plot $600
Bingo and lottery License	Town Clerk	• 2.5% of the total prizes awarded	Fee is waived for lotteries held within schools
Road Closing Permit	Town Clerk	• $400 per application	$200 for emergency stand-by
Hawkers and Peddlers	Town Clerk	• $200 per vendor	
Dog License	Town Clerk	• $30 per dog; • $20 if dog is sterilized	
Seasonal Camp License	Planning Officer	• $200 for initial application; • $100 per year annual fee plus $10 per camp site	
Taxi Cab License	Town Clerk	• $15 per driver; • $150 per broker	
Road cuts and driveway entrances	Planning Officer	• $1,000 deposit; • actual fee will depend on hours worked by municipality crew	Minimum fee $200
Sewer System Permit	Planning Officer	• $300 for new systems plus a $50 inspection fee; • $100 for reinspection after failure	$200 for appeals
Building Permit	Planning Officer	• $2,000 flat fee for residential buildings; • additional fees if subdivision of land is required; $5 per $1,000 of value for commercial buildings	
Burn Permit	Fire Department	• $300 per year; • $300 additional if more than one emergency call	

Note: These examples are fictitious, but reflect the structure of permit and licensing fees in a number of municipalities.

Case Analysis and Recommendation[3]

To: Mayor, Fairy Falls[4]

From: Chief Administrative Officer, Fairy Falls
Re: Review of Permit and License Fees

I have reviewed the current structure of our license and permit fees in light of your concerns about recent court decisions. I believe that we are not in compliance with the court's directive that these fees must reflect the actual cost of providing the services. In the memo below I will identify some potential problem areas, prioritize where we should make changes, and recommend a plan for undertaking these changes. I recommend that we undertake an activity-based costing study of the cost of providing permits and licenses, beginning with those affecting businesses.

A Review of Current Fee Structures

It is unlikely that our present system of permit and licensing fees reflects the costs of these services.[5] First, we know that these fees were originally set based on the fees used by neighboring municipalities. We did not use our costs at that time as a basis for setting fees. Second, the fees have been adjusted periodically with across-the-board percentage increases. Unless each permit and licensing process uses exactly the same resources, it is unlikely that the costs associated with different products would increase at the same rate. Finally, a quick review of our permit and license fees shows a variety of pricing models:

- variable fees (e.g., Bingo licenses, building permits)
- fixed fees (e.g., dog licenses, transient trader licenses, road closing permits)
- combination fixed and variable fees (e.g., trailer camp licenses, taxi cab licenses)

It seems unlikely, on the face of it, that these patterns of fees reflect the underlying pattern of costs. For example, our Bingo license fee varies with the value of the prize, but it seems likely that the cost of issuing and policing the license is virtually the same for each Bingo. In addition, some

---

[3] This is an example response to the case; other approaches may be possible.

[4] The response format chosen is a memo as this is a communication within the organization. The addressee is the mayor, but it is likely that the document will be shared with other members of council and possibly a wider public. This context means that the discussion must be presented in lay terms (i.e., no jargon should be used, and technical terms must be explained) and that care must be taken to set out options for the mayor and council to discuss and decide upon.

[5] In this case the issue has been identified by the mayor but the analysis first tries to judge whether or not this issue is actually present. If, for example, the CAO historically based recommendations for fees on costs, then the mayor's issue would disappear. This discussion provides three case facts that indicate the likelihood that a problem exists.

of our fees recur annually (e.g., trailer camp licenses) and we may not be providing an annual service that justifies these fees.

Overall, I believe that the relationship between our costs and our fees is subject to challenge. Furthermore, at present we would not be able to provide a cost-based justification for these fees.

Issues in Identifying Costs

Any attempt to link costs and fees will have to recognize some technical issues owing to the size of the municipality and the nature of the services we provide:[6]

- First, because of the seasonality of municipal operations, actual costs may vary depending on the time of year a service is provided. For example, in winter we may approve only one or two building permits per month,[7] whereas in spring we receive hundreds of applications per month. We need to decide whether we want to charge the actual cost of providing a service or the average cost over the year, as these costs will vary with the volume of work done.

- Second, we are a small municipality but we are required by law to provide basic services to our residents. This means that there are fixed costs associated with our activities (e.g., we have a full-time Town Clerk, whose salary does not vary depending on the number of permits issued), so the extra cost of processing a licensing application in this situation is zero (since we would have to pay the clerk's salary regardless of whether the application was made). This means that the marginal cost of providing services will differ dramatically from the full or average cost. We need to decide whether we want to charge the full cost of providing permits and licenses or the marginal cost.

Alternatives

A number of alternatives are available to Council that would address the problems raised by the court cases. These alternatives are discussed below in more detail.[8] The alternatives are as follows:

- Do nothing.
- Rearrange operations to make the costs of permits and licenses visible.

---

[6] These are situational constraints that will affect how costs can be estimated and that will establish a second issue — that "cost" does not refer to a single number so that linking fees to "cost" also means choosing which cost to use for this purpose.

[7] This is not a fact in the case, but rather a reasonable assumption given the seasonality of construction in Canada.

[8] The memo is designed as a decision tree to show the mayor what alternatives are available. The choices at the higher levels of the tree are policy decisions that should be taken by political representatives. The choices at lower levels of the tree are more technical decisions that the council would be happy to delegate to the staff.

- Undertake a costing study to identify the costs of permits and licenses under current operations. This option allows for two main variations regarding how the costs are to be calculated:
  - o Calculate full versus marginal costs.
  - o Calculate actual versus average (normal) costs.

One alternative is to do nothing. At the moment, while there are court rulings on the relationship between costs and fees, these are specific to particular instances and there is no requirement for us to act at this time. However, I appreciate that you, as Mayor, want to keep the Town at the forefront of municipal financial management, and it makes sense to anticipate the risk of court challenges to our fees.[9] I believe that we should be proactive in addressing this issue.

If we decide to act to align our costs with our fees, then we have two alternatives. First, we can arrange our activities so that the costs of providing permits and licenses are directly attributable to those processes.[10] This will make the costs visible and will meet the concerns regarding the relationship between costs and fees. Second, we can do cost studies to identify the costs of these activities as we are presently organized.

I do not believe that we can or should establish separate units for permits and licenses. Since we are a small municipality, many of our resources are shared among different functions. In addition, our permitting and licensing functions are spread among (at least) three different departments to take advantage of the specialized expertise associated with each department. We would not have the scale of operations to create separate units in each department to handle permits and licenses, and we do not have people with the range of skills and knowledge needed to bring all of these functions together in one unit. These constraints make the creation of a separate unit, or units, to deal with permits and licenses an inefficient way of handling the issue.

This discussion supports the alternative of developing a costing system to capture the costs of permits and licenses. There are many choices that can be made in designing a costing system, most of which are technical details that our staff will handle. There are two main choices, however, that you as Mayor and the Council may wish to consider.[11] First, we must decide whether we will charge the actual costs of each permit, or an average cost that ignores variations in cost over the year and that also ignores

---

[9] This sentence recognizes the mayor's objectives in undertaking the review and uses this to reject the alternative of doing nothing until challenged in the courts. This brief paragraph combines alternative generation, consequence evaluation, and a decision with regard to further consideration of the alternative.

[10] Many costing problems arise because the way a business is structured disguises the costs incurred. It is not unusual for a business to reorganize so that costs can be more easily recognized and managed. For example, firms may outsource services because of the lack of good internal information to judge their efficiency and effectiveness.

[11] The way the memo is formatted depends heavily on the role being taken. In this case the response from the CAO to the mayor crosses a line between operational and strategic issues. The response must identify the issues that have political consequences and leave those to the council, while identifying minor issues that will be handled internally.

minor (the meaning of "minor" will be discussed below) variations in the specifics of a permit or license application. Second, we need to decide whether we will calculate the full cost or the marginal cost of our services. I believe that we should be calculating the average (normal), full costs of permits and licenses.

It would be expensive to calculate the actual costs of providing services (i.e., each permit or license application would be billed according to the resources used), and these costs would vary widely over the year, resulting in incentives for people to delay their applications for permits and licenses until the busiest times of year, since the higher volume of activity would result in lower costs during those periods based on economies of scale. Also, our citizens expect to be treated equally by their municipality, and the cost of a permit should not vary depending on factors beyond their control.[12] This suggests that we should find the average cost of permits and licenses and set fees according to this cost. The only variation in these costs should relate to factors that the applicant can control. For example, a permit for a complex activity that requires hours of work by staff to review should be charged more than a simple permit, but the same permit submitted at different times of the year should not be charged differently. The costing study should help us identify which characteristics of permit and license applications cause us to incur more costs, and which variations can be considered minor and thus can be ignored in establishing our fee schedule.

Since in total our revenues must cover the expenses of the municipality, and the marginal cost of some resources involved in providing any single license or permit may be zero, the use of marginal costing would not allow us to fund the capacity needed to provide our services.[13] Full costing would ensure that we *can* cover these costs. This requires that we allocate a portion of our fixed costs (e.g., staff time) to permits and licenses. There are many cost allocation procedures that could be used for this purpose. Once you and the Council have agreed on the basis on which our costs should be calculated, the staff and I will design an appropriate system. Given the discussion above, however, it would be useful to follow allocation procedures that are based on the attributes of applications that cause variations in our cost of providing the service. Activity-based costing is one approach that focuses on the processes that generate costs, and it

---

[12] These two criteria are being introduced to help narrow the alternatives. The criteria are not explicit in the case but are reasonable given the context (i.e., a municipal government in which the usual rules regarding equal treatment of all citizens would apply).

[13] This point could be expanded to ensure that the distinction is clear. At the margin, each additional application requires no new resources, so in essence the cost of providing the service (the opportunity cost) is zero. But if we don't charge for any application, then we would have no funds to hire the people who provide those services (this is the classic public good problem in economics). The solution suggested here is to charge people in order to have the capacity available to process the application. This requires us to know the expected or average number of applications during the year and calculate the average cost accordingly.

would fit well with this situation.[14] This is probably the approach that we would use if the recommendation below is accepted.

Recommendation

I recommend that we conduct an activity-based costing (ABC) analysis to determine the average full costs of our services. An ABC analysis will identify the time spent by staff and the resources consumed to complete the processing of permits and licensing applications. The ABC analysis will begin by identifying the processes that are undertaken (e.g., hours of planning officer time spent on a building permit review), and identify the costs of those processes (e.g., the portion of the salary of the planning officer for the time spent), and then accumulate the costs to show the average full cost of our services. The process analysis will also show whether there are variations in the nature of permits and license applications that affect our costs and that should be reflected in our fee schedules. Although this approach requires judgment and represents an approximation of how resources will be consumed in the long run, assuming no changes in the underlying processes, it is systematic and well documented and thus will support any legal defense of our fees should this be necessary.[15]

Implementation Issues

Prior to undertaking the costing studies, I cannot say whether the costs of permits and licenses will increase or decrease. This has two consequences that the Council should recognize.[16] First, since permit and license fees are part of the municipality's revenues, a change in the fees charged may result in either a reduction or an increase in the other taxes we charge in order to make the changes revenue neutral overall (i.e., any increase or decrease in permit fees must be offset by a change in other taxes or by a change in expenses). Council should be aware of the political implications of this change.

---

[14] A judgment is required regarding how much detail about alternatives to present. In this response, the alternatives shown are those which will dramatically affect the fees charged and the likelihood that the fees will support the long-run cost of the services and be acceptable to the citizens (i.e., full versus marginal costs, actual versus normal costs). These alternatives are important to the mayor and council. The details of ABC are not important, but presenting this alternative in brief demonstrates how the costing will be implemented.

[15] This last sentence brings the recommendation back to the mayor's concern about the legal risk to which the town may be exposed by using fees that cannot be justified based on cost.

[16] The context of this case is important. The role of the CAO is to implement the policies of the Council, but the CAO needs also to apprise Council of any actions that may result in concerns by taxpayers. The Council represents taxpayers and needs to make decisions with their interests in mind, but in some cases decisions need to be taken that will have unavoidable impacts on taxpayers. In these cases the Council's role is to ensure that the need for the action is understood and that potential opposition to the plan is managed to allow the staff to function effectively.

Second, the changes in fees charged may affect the competitiveness of our permits relative to those of neighboring municipalities. If these changes are material, it may have positive or negative impacts on business decisions (e.g., builders may find it more or less expensive to build speculative homes in Fairy Falls if the cost of building permits, septic permits, and the like changes materially).

Since the possibility of court challenges to our fees by business was the initial motivation for your request, I also recommend that we begin this process with a study of those permits which are of largest absolute value and which have the most impact on businesses. I would prioritize building (and related) permits and business operating licenses. Minor permits such as burn permits and dog licenses can be left until more staff time is available for analysis.

One side effect of generating better information about the costs of our permits and licenses is that we will be able to manage those costs. I recommend that we put in place an activity-based management system to help ensure that we are providing these services as efficiently as possible, and that we benchmark our fees against those of other municipalities that have made the change to cost-based fee schedules.

Index

About the Author

Alan J. Richardson is Odette Research Chair and Professor of Accounting at the Odette School of Business, University of Windsor, Canada. He has also held positions at the Schulich School of Business, York University, University of Alberta, Queen's University and the Helsinki School of Economics. He holds a PhD from Queen's University and is a Certified General Accountant. He was awarded Life Membership in the Certified General Accountants of Ontario and Fellowship in the Certified General Accountants of Canada in recognition of his contributions to the accounting profession. In 2010 he received the L.S. Rosen Outstanding Accounting Educator Award:

> given by the Canadian Academic Accounting Association for Contributions to Canadian accounting education over a sustained period of time through: excellence in teaching, publications (books, educational material, case studies, articles in magazines, etc.), educational innovation, research guidance for graduate students, involvement in professional and academic societies and activities.

He has published two edited collections of teaching cases (in financial accounting and management accounting). He serves on the editorial boards of ten academic journals and was the founding editor of *Canadian Accounting Perspectives* (now *Accounting Perspectives*). His research focuses on the institutional structure of accounting practice. His work has been published in journals such as *Accounting Organizations and Society, Contemporary Accounting Research, Journal of Accounting Research and Accounting History* as well as in journals in cognate disciplines such as the *Journal of Applied Psychology, Work and Occupations*, the *Journal of Canadian Studies and the Canadian Journal of Sociology*.